GitLab Cookbook

Over 60 hands-on recipes to efficiently self-host your own
Git repository using GitLab

Jeroen van Baarsen

[PACKT] open source*
PUBLISHING   community experience distilled

BIRMINGHAM - MUMBAI

GitLab Cookbook

Copyright © 2014 Packt Publishing

First published: December 2014

Production reference: 1191214

Published by Packt Publishing Ltd.
Livery Place
35 Livery Street
Birmingham B3 2PB, UK.

ISBN 978-1-78398-684-2

www.packtpub.com

Credits

Author
Jeroen van Baarsen

Reviewers
Denis Fateyev
Bert JW Regeer
George C. Guvernator V

Commissioning Editor
Amarabha Banerjee

Acquisition Editor
Vinay Argekar

Content Development Editor
Susmita Sabat

Technical Editor
Sebastian Rodrigues

Copy Editors
Rashmi Sawant
Stuti Srivastava

Project Coordinator
Kartik Vedam

Proofreaders
Simran Bhogal
Maria Gould
Ameesha Green
Paul Hindle

Graphics
Abhinash Sahu

Indexer
Tejal Soni

Production Coordinator
Aparna Bhagat

Cover Work
Aparna Bhagat

About the Author

Jeroen van Baarsen started programming at the age of 14. His language of choice was PHP. He started his first programming job at the age of 16 and worked in several companies as a PHP developer before he found out about the wonderful language that Ruby is. He then started learning this language and took up a job as a Ruby developer.

Currently, he works at Firmhouse, which is a company that helps build foundations for innovations and new business. Firmhouse has created the Ruby on Rails hosting platform at `intercityup.com`.

In his spare time, he contributes to GitLab's open source core team as a member. He is responsible for the merge requests that are opened by the community.

I would like to thank my girlfriend for supporting me while I was writing this book.

About the Reviewers

Denis Fateyev holds a Master's degree in Computer Science and has been working with Linux for more than 10 years (mostly with RedHat and CentOS). Currently, he works as a Perl programmer and a DevOps for a small German company. As a keen participant of the open source community, he is a package maintainer on Fedora and Repoforge projects. Foreign languages (German and Spanish) and linguistics are his passion.

He can be reached at `denis@fateyev.com`.

Bert JW Regeer is a software and systems engineer who has a wide range of skills that allow him to solve interesting and difficult problems quickly and efficiently. An avid user and developer of open source software, he enjoys working with Unix and Unix-like operating systems and has vast knowledge of not only the operating system, but also all of the software that the open source community provides. Along with his open source accomplishments, Bert is an entrepreneur who has worked with various start-ups. He continues to look for the next challenge at every turn to not only hone his craft, but also continue learning about new ideas and technologies and how to apply them in the best manner.

Apart from technology, he enjoys building things, taking things apart, and traveling. He has visited amazing places and has taken in various cultures around the world, and he continues to marvel at human ingenuity and the beauty the world provides.

He can be reached at `bertjw@regeer.org`.

George C. Guvernator V (Quint) studies computer science and linguistics at the College of William and Mary in Virginia. He is due to receive his BS in both fields in 2017. He has worked with the University of Colorado, Colorado Springs, where he researched machine learning in technical design. He is currently developing a study with the William and Mary makerspace to advance adaptive and assistive technology using augmented reality audio. Quint works as a web developer with the Institute for the Theory and Practice of International Relations, designs sound and music for short films and games, and edits the William and Mary student newspaper. Apart from his studies, Quint enjoys hiking, open source, cooking, and making music.

www.PacktPub.com

Support files, eBooks, discount offers, and more

For support files and downloads related to your book, please visit www.PacktPub.com.

Did you know that Packt offers eBook versions of every book published, with PDF and ePub files available? You can upgrade to the eBook version at www.PacktPub.com and as a print book customer, you are entitled to a discount on the eBook copy. Get in touch with us at service@packtpub.com for more details.

At www.PacktPub.com, you can also read a collection of free technical articles, sign up for a range of free newsletters and receive exclusive discounts and offers on Packt books and eBooks.

https://www2.packtpub.com/books/subscription/packtlib

Do you need instant solutions to your IT questions? PacktLib is Packt's online digital book library. Here, you can search, access, and read Packt's entire library of books.

Why Subscribe?

- ▶ Fully searchable across every book published by Packt
- ▶ Copy and paste, print, and bookmark content
- ▶ On demand and accessible via a web browser

Free Access for Packt account holders

If you have an account with Packt at www.PacktPub.com, you can use this to access PacktLib today and view 9 entirely free books. Simply use your login credentials for immediate access.

Table of Contents

Preface

GitLab is a popular, open source Git hosting solution implemented by more than 50,000 organizations. Over the last few years, GitLab has evolved with strong community support and growth, handling thousands of users on a single server and several such servers on an active cluster. If you need to set up a Git server, GitLab provides a perfect solution for you!

This book has some carefully chosen recipes to help you decide on the type of GitLab installation that will fit your requirements. You will also explore the benefits of each of these installation types.

Along with covering some of the basic principles of Git, the book covers practical scenarios that will show how you or your organization can effectively manage your proprietary code. You will learn how to manage multiple users, groups, and the permissions GitLab has for them. Updating your GitLab instance, creating backups, and restoring backups are some of the important tasks that are described in detail in order to assist you in maintaining your GitLab server. Moreover, the GitLab API is extensively covered to guide you through the various operations to help you manage your project. Among some of the more complex stuff, you will see how to incorporate the Git workflow and integrate GitLab in your existing LDAP environment. Furthermore, the book takes a peek at the GitLab CI, which is a continuous integration service specially built by people from GitLab for GitLab.

To summarize, this Cookbook will provide you with the knowledge required to work effortlessly toward self-hosting your Git repositories and maintaining them. Whether you are dealing with small or large projects, the recipes conveniently provide you with a thorough learning curve to help you handle the repository with speed and efficiency.

What this book covers

Chapter 1, Introduction and Installation, looks at the different ways in which you can install GitLab. We will also create your first project on your own GitLab server.

Chapter 2, Explaining Git, looks at the basics of Git, how to send your code to your GitLab server, how to get your GitLab project on your computer, and how to squash your commits into one nice commit.

Chapter 3, Managing Users, Groups, and Permissions, looks at how you can add new users and what the different permissions that you can grant your users are. We will also look at the power of GitLab groups.

Chapter 4, Issue Tracker and Wiki, shows how GitLab has a powerful issue tracker and wiki system. In this chapter, we will take a look at how you can get the most out of it.

Chapter 5, Maintaining Your GitLab Instance, shows how you need to maintain a GitLab instance and update backups when running them. We will look it all up!

Chapter 6, Webhooks, External Services, and the API, looks at webhooks and shows how you can test them. We will look at linking your GitLab system to external services such as project management tools, and we will look at the powerful API that GitLab ships with.

Chapter 7, Using LDAP and OmniAuth Providers, looks at how you can use your LDAP infrastructure to manage your GitLab users. We will also look at how to use external authentication methods called OmniAuth providers.

Chapter 8, GitLab CI, talks about GitLab having a powerful Continuous Integration system. In this chapter, we will look at how you can install and link it to your GitLab server.

Appendix, Tips and Tricks, looks at some smaller tasks, tips, and tricks that can help you in your daily GitLab usage.

What you need for this book

In this book, we will use a server to which you can install GitLab, so you need to have a server, VPS, or Virtual Machine with at least the following specifications:

- Ubuntu 12.03 64-bit or newer
- A CPU with one or two cores
- 1 GB RAM or 2 GB

For most of the recipes, you also need a working Internet connection, as you need to download certain packages.

Who this book is for

This book is intended for developers and DevOps that have a GitLab server running and want to be sure that they use it to the fullest. It is also aimed at people who are looking for a great Git platform and want to learn how to set it up successfully. Some system administrating skills on a Unix-based system are preferred but not required.

Sections

In this book, you will find several headings that appear frequently (Getting ready, How to do it, How it works, There's more, and See also).

To give clear instructions on how to complete a recipe, we use these sections as follows:

Getting ready

This section tells you what to expect in the recipe, and describes how to set up any software or any preliminary settings required for the recipe.

How to do it...

This section contains the steps required to follow the recipe.

How it works...

This section usually consists of a detailed explanation of what happened in the previous section.

There's more...

This section consists of additional information about the recipe in order to make the reader more knowledgeable about the recipe.

See also

This section provides helpful links to other useful information for the recipe.

Conventions

In this book, you will find a number of styles of text that distinguish between different kinds of information. Here are some examples of these styles, and an explanation of their meaning.

Code words in text, database table names, folder names, filenames, file extensions, pathnames, dummy URLs, user input, and Twitter handles are shown as follows: "You can now log in with the username `root` and password `5iveL!fe`."

A block of code is set as follows:

```
production: &base
  gitlab:
    port: 80
```

When we wish to draw your attention to a particular part of a code block, the relevant lines or items are set in bold:

```
[core]
        editor = 'vim'
```

Any command-line input or output is written as follows:

```
$ sudo gitlab-ctl restart
```

New terms and **important words** are shown in bold. Words that you see on the screen, in menus or dialog boxes for example, appear in the text like this: "Postfix will ask you what kind of installation you want; choose the **Internet Site** option."

 Warnings or important notes appear in a box like this.

 Tips and tricks appear like this.

Reader feedback

Feedback from our readers is always welcome. Let us know what you think about this book—what you liked or may have disliked. Reader feedback is important for us to develop titles that you really get the most out of.

To send us general feedback, simply send an e-mail to feedback@packtpub.com, and mention the book title via the subject of your message.

If there is a topic that you have expertise in and you are interested in either writing or contributing to a book, see our author guide on www.packtpub.com/authors.

Customer support

Now that you are the proud owner of a Packt book, we have a number of things to help you to get the most from your purchase.

Errata

Although we have taken every care to ensure the accuracy of our content, mistakes do happen. If you find a mistake in one of our books—maybe a mistake in the text or the code—we would be grateful if you would report this to us. By doing so, you can save other readers from frustration and help us improve subsequent versions of this book. If you find any errata, please report them by visiting http://www.packtpub.com/submit-errata, selecting your book, clicking on the **errata submission form** link, and entering the details of your errata. Once your errata are verified, your submission will be accepted and the errata will be uploaded on our website, or added to any list of existing errata, under the Errata section of that title. Any existing errata can be viewed by selecting your title from http://www.packtpub.com/support.

Piracy

Piracy of copyright material on the Internet is an ongoing problem across all media. At Packt, we take the protection of our copyright and licenses very seriously. If you come across any illegal copies of our works, in any form, on the Internet, please provide us with the location address or website name immediately so that we can pursue a remedy.

Please contact us at copyright@packtpub.com with a link to the suspected pirated material.

We appreciate your help in protecting our authors, and our ability to bring you valuable content.

Questions

You can contact us at questions@packtpub.com if you are having a problem with any aspect of the book, and we will do our best to address it.

1
Introduction and Installation

In this chapter, we will cover the following recipes:

- ▶ Using the Omnibus package
- ▶ Setting up the server dependencies for source installation
- ▶ Setting up the database for source installation
- ▶ Installing GitLab from source
- ▶ Using Chef and GitLab Cookbook
- ▶ Logging in for the first time
- ▶ Creating your first project

Introduction

GitLab is a self-hosted system for managing your code. It was first released in October 2011, and is updated every twenty-second day of the month since then. It was released under the MIT license.

It used to be hosted on GitHub, but since January 2014, its main source of hosting is gitlab.com. The fork of GitLab, which is hosted on GitHub, will remain active as a source where you can file issues and merge requests.

GitLab was founded by Dmitriy Zaporozhets in 2013. He has worked on GitLab full-time since 2013. The project consists of two main groups: on one side, the open source core team, and on the other side, the GitLab B.V. team (the second one is the company side of GitLab).

Besides the amazing project management tool for Git projects, the GitLab **Continuous Integration** (**CI**) system also exists; this is a CI system that highly integrates with GitLab.

In this book, we will be using the **Community Edition** (**CE**) of GitLab. The CE version is the free open source version that you can download. There is also an enterprise version. The enterprise version includes a support subscription where the GitLab B.V. team helps you with problems with the installation of it.

If you want to give GitLab a try, or just don't want to host it yourself, take a look at `gitlab.com`. You can find the hosted version of GitLab there. It's run by the team behind GitLab B.V., so you know you're in good hands!

Using the Omnibus package

The people from GitLab have created an Omnibus package for the major Linux distributions (Ubuntu, Debian, and CentOS). These packages are an easy way of installing your GitLab installation, as they have all the dependencies packaged with them.

For this recipe, we are going to use the Ubuntu version of the Omnibus package.

Getting ready

Before we start installing, you need to have a server installed with a Ubuntu 12.04 64-bit system, and have SSH access to the server.

How to do it...

Here is how you can install GitLab using Omnibus:

1. Download the package, change the `X.Y.Z` portion to the version you want to download. At the time of writing, 7.3.2 is the latest version:

    ```
    wget https://downloads-packages.s3.amazonaws.com/ubuntu-
    12.04/gitlab_X.Y.Z-omnibus.5.1.0.ci-1_amd64.deb
    ```

2. Install the OpenSSH server:

    ```
    sudo apt-get install openssh-server
    ```

3. Install Postfix:

    ```
    sudo apt-get install postfix
    ```

4. Postfix will ask you what kind of installation you want; choose the **Internet Site** option.

5. Enter the fully qualified domain name for the domain you want GitLab to send e-mails from (that is, `gitlab.example.com`).

6. Install the Omnibus package, and replace the `X.Y.Z` part with your version:

   `sudo dpkg -i gitlab_7.3.2-omnibus.5.1.0.ci-1_amd64.deb`

7. Now, we will configure your GitLab instance by running the following command:

   `sudo gitlab-ctl reconfigure`

8. Check to see whether all the services are running using the following command:

   `sudo gitlab-ctl status`

   The output should look like the following screenshot:

```
run: nginx: (pid 2499) 359s; run: log: (pid 2498) 359s
run: postgresql: (pid 2415) 389s; run: log: (pid 2414) 389s
run: redis: (pid 2333) 395s; run: log: (pid 2332) 395s
run: sidekiq: (pid 2484) 365s; run: log: (pid 2483) 365s
run: unicorn: (pid 2473) 367s; run: log: (pid 2472) 367s
```

You can now log in with the username `root` and password `5iveL!fe`.

How it works...

We have just installed GitLab via the Omnibus installer. Omnibus is a way to package your application and install all the dependencies that are required to run it.

GitLab makes good use of this capability. As you only have to install a mail server and an OpenSSH server, all the other parts are automatically installed for you.

GitLab will auto configure itself with the recommended settings. If you want to change your configuration, you have to first create the configuration file. You can do this as follows:

```
$ sudo mkdir -p /etc/gitlab
$ sudo touch /etc/gitlab/gitlab.rb
$ sudo chmod 600 /etc/gitlab/gitlab.rb
```

The settings that you are most likely to change are the ones that are in the `gitlab.yml` file (`https://gitlab.com/gitlab-org/gitlab-ce/blob/master/config/gitlab.yml.example`).

You need to make a small translation change in order to make this work, so let's say you want to change the port that GitLab is running on; normally, you would change the port value in the GitLab file, but now you have to add an entry to `/etc/gitlab/gitlab.rb`.

So, for the port, the entry in `gitlab.yml` would look like the following code:

```
production: &base
  gitlab:
    port: 80
```

In the `gitlab.rb` file, you need to create the following entry: `gitlab_rails['port'] = 80`.

Setting up the server dependencies for source installation

To install GitLab from source, we need to install some dependencies on the server. Besides installing the required packages, we will also create the user that will serve our GitLab installation.

How to do it...

The installation procedure is applicable for Debian-based systems only. GitLab also supports other Linux distributions, but the installation process is a bit different. For more information, visit the `gitlab.com` website. Perform the following steps:

1. Install the required packages using the following command:

    ```
    $ sudo apt-get install -y build-essential zlib1g-dev libyaml-dev libssl-dev libgdbm-dev libreadline-dev libncurses5-dev libffi-dev curl openssh-server redis-server checkinstall libxml2-dev libxslt-dev libcurl4-openssl-dev libicu-dev logrotate
    ```

2. Install Ruby using the following commands:

    ```
    $ mkdir /tmp/ruby && cd /tmp/ruby
    ```

    ```
    $ curl --progress ftp://ftp.ruby-lang.org/pub/ruby/2.0/ruby-2.0.0-p481.tar.gz | tar xz cd ruby-2.0.0-p481
    ```

    ```
    $ ./configure --disable-install-rdoc
    ```

    ```
    $ make
    ```

    ```
    $ sudo make install
    ```

3. Install the Bundler gem:

    ```
    $ sudo gem install bundler --no-ri --no-rdoc
    ```

4. Create the Git user:

    ```
    $ sudo adduser --disabled-login --gecos 'GitLab' git
    ```

How it works...

At this point, we have installed the server dependencies and installed Ruby on our system. We also installed the Bundler gem; `bundler` is the package manager for Ruby, and as GitLab is written in Ruby, this one will be very important later on, so we can download all the dependencies for GitLab.

The Git user was created so that GitLab and all its dependencies can run under its own user; that way, it is possible to sandbox the installation better and make sure that our system stays secure.

Set up the database for source installation

GitLab can be installed using PostgreSQL or MySQL. In this recipe, I will use PostgreSQL as it is the recommended database engine.

How to do it...

The following steps are applicable for Debian-based systems; they are also possible with RedHat. You can take a look at `gitlab.com` for the installation instructions.

1. Install PostgreSQL 9.1:

    ```
    sudo apt-get install -y postgresql-9.1 postgresql-client
    libpq-dev
    ```

2. Create the PostgreSQL user for GitLab:

    ```
    sudo -u  postgresql psql -d template1 -c "CREATE USER git
    CREATEDB"
    ```

3. Create the database for GitLab and grant all privileges on the database:

    ```
    sudo -u postgresql psql -d template1 -c "CREATE DATABASE
    gitlabhq_production OWNER git"
    ```

Installing GitLab from source

In this recipe, I will help you install GitLab from source. Installing from source means that we will take the source code from `gitlab.com` and use that to code in order to install it on our server.

At the time of writing, 7.4 is the latest version. If you want to be sure that you have the latest version, please check `https://gitlab.com/gitlab-org/gitlab-ce/blob/master/VERSION`.

If you want the latest bleeding edge version, you can change 7.4 to master in this recipe.

Getting ready

To install GitLab on your own server, you need to have a few things installed already. Here is a list of prerequisites:

- A server running Debian or Ubuntu; preferably one of the latest versions, and running as 64-bit
- Git Version 1.7 or higher
- A text editor; in the examples, I'll be using Vim
- Sudo; on Debian this is not installed by default
- A working mail server
- You have to set up the database
- You have to install all the server dependencies

How to do it...

Follow these steps to install GitLab from source:

1. Download the source code:

```
$ cd /home/git
$ sudo -u git -H git clone https://gitlab.com/gitlab-
org/gitlab-ce.git -b 6-9-stable gitlab
```

2. In `config/gitlab.yml`, we need to change the host to the fully-qualified domain name of your GitLab instance. Also change the `email_from` to the e-mail address you want to use as a from address for all the e-mails that are sent by GitLab:

```
$ cd /home/git/gitlab
$ sudo -u git -H cp config/gitlab.yml.example
config/gitlab.yml
$ sudo -u git -H editor config/gitlab.yml
```

3. Make sure that GitLab can write to the necessary folders using the following command lines:

```
$ sudo chown -R git log/
$ sudo chown -R git tmp/
$ sudo chmod -R u+rwX log/
$ sudo chmod -R u+rwX tmp/
$ sudo chmod -R u+rwX tmp/pids/
$ sudo chmod -R u+rwX tmp/sockets/
$ sudo chmod -R u+rwX  public/uploads
```

4. Create the directory for the GitLab satellites:

```
$ sudo -u git -H mkdir /home/git/gitlab-satellites
$ sudo chmod u+rwx,g+rx,o-rwx /home/git/gitlab-satellites
```

5. Copy the Unicorn config file:

```
$ sudo -u git -H cp config/unicorn.rb.example
config/unicorn.rb
```

6. Copy the Rack attack config file:

```
$ sudo -u git -H cp config/initializers/rack_attack.rb.example
config/initializers/rack_attack.rb
```

7. Copy the `init` script and make GitLab start on boot:

```
$ sudo cp lib/support/init.d/gitlab /etc/init.d/gitlab
$ sudo update-rc.d gitlab defaults 21
```

8. Set up Logrotate:

```
$ sudo cp lib/support/logrotate/gitlab /etc/logrotate.d/gitlab
```

9. Set up the Git user. This helps when editing files via the GitLab web interface. Make sure that the `user.email` is the same as the e-mail address you entered in step 8:

```
$ sudo -u git -H git config --global user.name "GitLab"
$ sudo -u git -H git config --global user.email
"example@example.com"
$ sudo -u git -H git config --global core.autocrlf input
```

10. Configure your GitLab database:

```
$ sudo -u git -H cp config/database.yml.postgresql
config/database.yml
```

11. Make sure that the `database.yml` file is only readable for the `git` user:

```
$ sudo -u git -H chmod o-rwx config/database.yml
```

12. Install the GitLab dependencies:

```
$ sudo -u git -H bundle install --deployment --without
development test mysql aws
```

13. Install the GitLab shell:

```
$ sudo -u git -H bundle exec rake gitlab:shell:install[v1.9.4]
REDIS_URL=redis://localhost:6379 RAILS_ENV=production
```

14. Initialize the database:

```
$ sudo -u git -H bundle exec rake gitlab:setup
RAILS_ENV=production force=yes
```

15. Compile all the assets:

```
$ sudo -u git -H bundle exec rake assets:precompile
RAILS_ENV=production
```

16. Start your GitLab instance:

```
$ sudo /etc/init.d/gitlab restart
```

How it works...

We have just installed GitLab on our server. We have done this by downloading the source code from `gitlab.com` and performing the preceding steps.

Let's take a look at what we did in every step.

In step 1, we downloaded the source code for GitLab. We haven't done anything with it yet, just downloaded it.

In step 2, we done the basic configuration of GitLab. We have changed the hostname to the fully-qualified domain name you want to access your GitLab on, for example, `gitlab.example.com`. Also, we have configured the e-mail addresses that GitLab will send mails from. The `email_from` will be used as the from address of all the e-mails that are sent via GitLab.

Next was the setup for the satellite directory. Satellites are used when you create a merge request, and GitLab has to check whether it is mergeable, and perform the actual merge. A satellite is just checking out of the repository that GitLab has access to.

We then went on to copy some files. The first file was the Unicorn configuration file. Unicorn was used as the application server and we copied the Rack Attack files. Rack Attack is used in order to prevent abusive requests to your GitLab server. One way to make sure that no harmful requests make it to your server is by request throttling. This means that we only allow 10 requests per 60 seconds to certain URLs.

The next important step is the configuration of the database. As we are using PostgreSQL on the same machine, the configuration is really straightforward: just copy the right `database.yml` file and we are done, well almost; we also need to protect our `database.yml` file so that it's only readable for the Git user.

The dependency installation is done via Bundler. Bundler is the package manager for Ruby. We have passed the flags `--deployment` and `--without development test mysql aws`. The first flag is passed to make sure that the dependencies are installed in the context of GitLab and not in a system-wide context. The second flag is passed to make sure that only the necessary dependencies are installed. If you want to learn more about Bundler, take a look at `www.bundler.io`.

GitLab has its own Git wrapper to perform Git commands on the server. This wrapper is called GitLab Shell. In step 11, we tell GitLab to fetch the code for GitLab Shell and install it.

In step 12, we set up the database. We create the database and load the database schema. We also create the first user, so that you can log in to your server.

Using Chef and GitLab Cookbook

You can install GitLab using chef-solo. It allows you to install a server and all of its dependencies through a pre-programmed script. GitLab Cookbook is also used as the base for the Omnibus Package.

If you want more information on Chef, please take a look at www.getchef.com.

For this recipe, we are going to use a Ubuntu-based installation.

Getting ready

Before we start installing, you need to have a server installed with Ubuntu and have SSH access to the server. Your server needs to have at least 2 GB of RAM to compile all the requirements.

How to do it...

1. We start with downloading some server dependencies:

   ```
   sudo apt-get update && sudo apt-get install -y build-essential
   git curl
   ```

2. Download the chef-solo file:

   ```
   curl -o /tmp/solo.json https://gitlab.com/gitlab-org/cookbook-
   gitlab/raw/master/solo.json.production_example
   ```

3. We have to edit the file we just downloaded so that it fits our needs:

   ```
   vi /tmp/solo.json
   ```

4. As we will be using PostgreSQL, you can remove the MySQL part. Also, make sure you change the revision to the latest stable branch, 7.3 at time of writing. After you are done, your file should look like the following code, but with your own host and e-mail addresses:

   ```
   "gitlab": {
     "host": "gitlab.example.com",
     "url": "http://gitlab.example.com/",
     "email_from": "gitlab@example.com",
     "support_email": "support@gitlab.example.com",
     "database_adapter": "postgresql",
   ```

```
      "database_password": "super-secure-password",
      "revision": "6-9-stable"
    },
    "postgresql": {
      "password": {
        "postgres": "psqlpass"
      }
    },
    "postfix": {
      "mail_type": "client",
      "myhostname": "gitlab.example.com",
      "mydomain": "mydomain.com",
      "myorigin": "gitlab.example.com",
      "smtp_use_tls": "no"
    },
    "run_list": [
      "postfix",
      "gitlab::default"
    ]
}
```

5. Next, we download and install Chef to our server:

    ```
    cd /tmp; curl -LO https://www.opscode.com/chef/install.sh;
    sudo bash ./install.sh -v 11.4.4; sudo
    /opt/chef/embedded/bin/gem install berkshelf --no-ri --no-rdoc
    ```

6. Now, we download the GitLab source from `gitlab.com`:

    ```
    git clone https://gitlab.com/gitlab-org/cookbook-gitlab.git
    /tmp/cookbook-gitlab
    ```

7. Install all the GitLab-specific dependencies:

    ```
    cd /tmp/cookbook-gitlab; /opt/chef/embedded/bin/berks vendor
    /tmp/cookbooks
    ```

8. We need to create one more Chef config file:

    ```
    vi /tmp/solo.rb
    ```

9. Add the following content to the preceding config file:

    ```
    cookbook_path     ["/tmp/cookbooks/"]
    log_level         :debug
    ```

10. Save the file.

11. We are done with configuring everything and now let's install GitLab!

    ```
    sudo chef-solo -c /tmp/solo.rb -j /tmp/solo.json
    ```

How it works...

We just installed GitLab via the Chef cookbook. This way of installation is a little more automated than the installation from source, but it still gives you a bit more control over your installation in comparison to the Omnibus package.

Let's go through the steps that we took to install GitLab in this way.

First, we had to install some server dependencies that were needed to install Chef, and we also cloned the code from GitLab. The dependencies included Curl and Git. We used Curl to download the `chef.json` file, and in step 4, to download the check installation file. Git was needed to clone the source of GitLab, and to make sure that GitLab, when installed, is able to serve your repositories.

Next, we had to download the `config.json` file. This JSON file keeps the configuration information for GitLab in order to install itself. You can compare this to the `gitlab.yml` file from the *Installing GitLab from source* recipe.

In this recipe, we installed GitLab using PostgreSQL. If you'd prefer to install it with MySQL, that's possible. Just keep in mind that PostgreSQL is the recommended way of running GitLab.

The next step was to download the GitLab source and to install the GitLab dependencies. After we had done that, we created the `solo.rb` file. This file is used by chef-solo to know where GitLab Cookbook is located.

The last step was to install GitLab itself. This step took a while because the command also downloaded and compiled Ruby for you.

Logging in for the first time

When you have installed your server, you need to log in. GitLab comes with a built-in administrator account.

How to do it...

In this recipe, we will log in and create our own administrator account as follows:

1. Go to your domain where GitLab is installed (that is, `gitlab.example.com`).
2. Log in using the username `root` and password `5iveL!fe`.
3. You need to choose a new password; pick whatever you like.
4. Log in with the new information.

5. Go to the **Admin area** section, as shown in the following screenshot:

6. Navigate to **Users | New User**.
7. Fill in the information to create your own user. Don't forget to check the **Admin** checkbox.
8. Now, click on **Create user**.

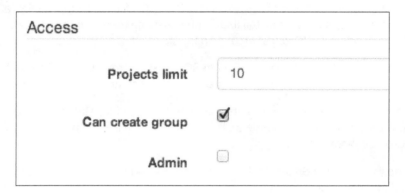

An e-mail will be sent to the given e-mail address. This e-mail will contain the new password for this account.

9. Log out from GitLab and log in with your new account.
10. You need to choose a new password and log in again.
11. Go to the **Admin area** section and click on **Users**.
12. Click on **Block** for the administrator account.

How it works...

As GitLab ships with a default administrator account, this makes it a bit unsecure by default. Therefore, when you don't change anything about your setup, everyone will be able to log in.

To ensure that we have a secure GitLab installation, we created a new administrator account, and gave it an administrator access. We also want to be sure that the default shipped account is not useable anymore, so that's why we logged in with our own account and disabled the account given by GitLab.

We had to log out first, as GitLab does not allow us to disable the account that is currently logged in.

Creating your first project

In this recipe, we will take a look at creating a project, and what the different visibility options are. The difficult part for people new to GitLab is the different visibility levels that GitLab offers. There are three visibility levels: private, internal, and public. They are explained as follows:

- **Private projects**: When you set the visibility to `Private`, the only people who can see this project are the people that you have granted access to this project, or those people who are members of the project's group.

- **Internal projects**: This will cause the project to be visible to all the users who have an account on your GitLab server.

- **Public projects**: GitLab offers a public access directory for projects when you choose Public for your project. This will be visible to everyone who knows the location of your GitLab server. When someone who has no account on your GitLab server views this project, they will have guest permissions.

The visibility level has nothing to do with the permissions someone has on your project. So, when you list your project as `Internal`, it does not mean that every user can change whatever they want. It just means that users who have an account can clone the project, and view issues and such.

You can always change the visibility of your project after you have created it. Just perform the following steps:

1. Go to your project dashboard.
2. Click on the **Edit** button.
3. Change the **Visibility level** option.

How to do it...

Follow these steps to create your project:

1. Click on the **New Project** button on the right-hand side, as shown in the following screenshot:

2. Fill in the project title. Let's pick Cookbook.
3. You can fill in an optional description.
4. Choose visibility level as **Private**.
5. Click on **Create Project**.

2
Explaining Git

In this chapter, we will cover the following recipes:

- ▸ Generating your SSH key on Unix-like systems
- ▸ Generating your SSH key on Windows
- ▸ Adding your SSH key to GitLab
- ▸ Creating your first Git project
- ▸ Cloning your repository and pushing code to it
- ▸ Working with branches
- ▸ Performing a rebase
- ▸ Squashing your commits

Introduction

Before you can use GitLab, you need to know a little about Git itself, what Git is, and what pushing code is. As Git is a very complex system and is worthy of a book of its own, I'm just going to cover the basics. You'll learn how to get your SSH key and how to push your first code to GitLab.

Git is in the heart of GitLab. Without it, there would be no GitLab. It is a super powerful source control system, and has some amazing features. We will take a look at some of those feature in this chapter.

In this chapter, I'll assume that you will be using Git over SSH. However, most recipes will work even if you use Git over HTTP.

If you want to learn more about Git, I recommend that you follow the `try.github.io` course. It's a free online workshop, and you will learn everything related to Git in an interactive way.

Generating your SSH key on Unix-like systems

Generating an SSH key on Linux and OS X is easy; they come with a built-in tool to do this, called `ssh-keygen`.

How to do it...

In the following steps, we will create an SSH key for your Unix system:

1. First, we are going to check whether you have any SSH keys present. Open your terminal and enter the following command:

    ```
    $ ls ~/.ssh
    ```

2. If you have a file named `id_rsa.pub` or `id_dsa.pub`, you can skip this recipe.

3. To generate a new SSH key, you need to open your terminal and enter the following command:

    ```
    $ ssh-keygen -t rsa -C "Comment for key"
    ```

    The comment can be anything you want; it makes it easier for you to see which key it is when you open the key file.

4. Now, we get to the question of what you want to name your key. Just press *Enter*.

5. You will be asked to enter a passphrase. Enter it, and be sure to choose a strong password.

You should see the following screenshot:

```
○ ○ ○                      1. jeroen@earth: ~ (zsh)
➜  ~  ssh-keygen -t rsa -C "book@example.com"
Generating public/private rsa key pair.
Enter file in which to save the key (/Users/jeroen/.ssh/id_rsa): id_rsa_book
Enter passphrase (empty for no passphrase):
Enter same passphrase again:
Your identification has been saved in id_rsa_book.
Your public key has been saved in id_rsa_book.pub.
The key fingerprint is:
5d:50:36:f8:60:36:ef:e3:9d:bc:1e:d5:7d:e7:70:f0 book@example.com
The key's randomart image is:
+--[ RSA 2048]----+
|        .o+      |
|        *o .     |
|       o =. .    |
|      . .o  oo|  |
|      S ..  . E|  |
|         o  =o|  |
|        . +...|  |
|         . +. |  |
|          .o. |  |
+-----------------+
➜  ~ []
```

Your SSH key is now generated.

How it works...

We just created our personal SSH key: one key is the `id_rsa` file and one is the `id_rsa.pub` file. Whenever you need to provide your public SSH key, make sure that you use the `id_rsa.pub` file. The other file should remain safely on your machine, as this is the private key. If you feel this key has been compromised, you should create a new SSH key and revoke the SSH key on all the systems you used it for.

The SSH key helps you to authorize yourself in your GitLab instance without having to use a username and password.

One thing that is important while creating your SSH key is to remember to enter a passphrase. We use an SSH key because we believe that passwords are less secure, so you might think that if you're using an SSH key, you will be safe. This is not entirely true. When a person takes control over your private key, they have access to every system you have put your public key in. However, when you use a passphrase for your SSH key, not only do they have to steal your private key, but they also know the password that goes with it.

Generating your SSH key on Windows

As Windows does not have a fully functioning terminal, we have to take some other steps to install Git and generate our SSH key. We will take a look at how this is done in this recipe.

How to do it...

1. Go to `http://git-scm.com/downloads` and click on Windows.

2. The download will start automatically. When it's done, you see the following installation window:

3. Click on **Next** and accept the license agreement.
4. Choose where you want to install Git and click on **Next**.
5. You will want the following components to be selected:

    ❑ **Windows Explorer integration**

    ❑ **Associate .git* configuration files with the default text editor**

    ❑ **Associate .sh files to be run with Bash**

After selecting the preceding components, click on **Next**. The following screenshot shows you these options:

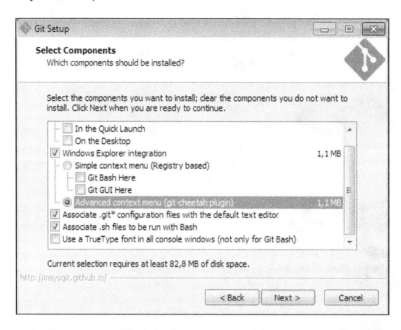

6. Choose where you want to place Git in your start menu and click on **Next**.

7. Choose **Use Git from Git Bash only** and click on **Next**.

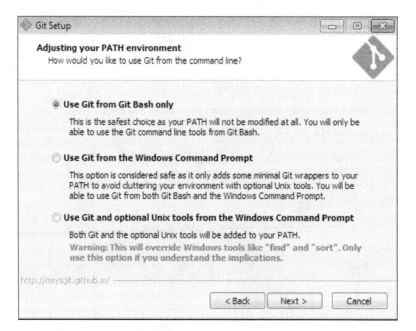

8. Select **Checkout Windows-style, commit Unix-style line endings**, and click on **Next**.

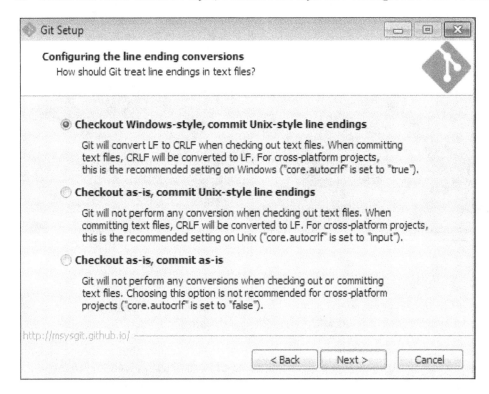

9. Wait until the installation is done and click on **Finish**.

10. Go to your start menu and open **Git Bash**. This will open the following terminal window:

11. To generate your SSH key, enter the following command:

```
ssh-keygen
```

12. When asked for the location at which you want to save the file, just press *Enter*.

13. Enter a secure passphrase for your SSH key.

14. Your SSH key is now generated, as shown in the following screenshot:

```
MINGW32:/c/Users/jeroen                                          [_][□][x]
jeroen@JEROEN-PC ~
$ ssh-keygen
Generating public/private rsa key pair.
Enter file in which to save the key (/c/Users/jeroen/.ssh/id_rsa):
Created directory '/c/Users/jeroen/.ssh'.
Enter passphrase (empty for no passphrase):
Enter same passphrase again:
Your identification has been saved in /c/Users/jeroen/.ssh/id_rsa.
Your public key has been saved in /c/Users/jeroen/.ssh/id_rsa.pub.
The key fingerprint is:
ab:ef:a7:3f:f7:8e:04:a8:71:c6:54:a6:91:0e:95:c4 jeroen@JEROEN-PC

jeroen@JEROEN-PC ~
$
```

How it works...

As Windows doesn't come with a built-in Git setup, we have to install it ourselves. We also have to install Git Bash so that we can use Git via the command line.

One thing that is important while creating your SSH key is to remember to enter a passphrase. We use an SSH key because we believe that passwords are less secure. So, you might think that if you're using an SSH key, you will be safe. That's not entirely true. When a person takes control over your private key, they have access to every system you have put your public key in. However, when you use a passphrase for your SSH key, not only do they have to steal your private key, but also know the password that goes with it.

Adding your SSH key to GitLab

In order for GitLab to know who we are and check whether we are authorized to commit certain code, we use our SSH key. The combination of the public key and the private key can tell GitLab that we are authorized, and GitLab will allow the operation to be performed.

How to do it...

To set up your SSH key, perform the following steps:

1. Open GitLab and go to your account settings.

2. Click on **SSH**.
3. Click on **Add SSH Key**.

4. To get information about your SSH key, enter the following command in your terminal. If you're using Windows, go to step 7:

    ```
    $ cat ~/.ssh/id_rsa.pub
    ```

5. You should copy the entire content of the output in step 4, as shown in the following screenshot:

6. If you're not using Windows, you can move to step 11.

7. Open the Windows explorer and move to `C:\Users\your_username\.ssh`.

8. Right-click on **id_rsa.pub** and click on **Open**.

9. When asked for the program you want to use, select **Notepad**.

10. Select the entire content of the file that contains the SSH key.

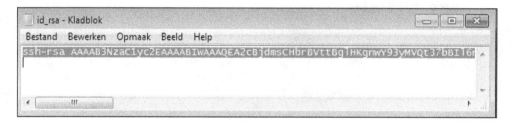

11. We now paste the content of the SSH key into the form in your GitLab instance. You can name the SSH key anything you want. It is recommended that you name it after the computer it came from. This way, it will be easier to know which key belongs to which machine. If you leave the name field empty, GitLab will generate a name for you.

12. Now, click on **Add Key**.

How it works...

In order to make Git aware of your SSH key, you need to add the public portion of the key to GitLab. When you add the SSH key to GitLab, it will put the key for the Git user in the `authorized_keys` file on the GitLab server.

Whenever you will execute a Git command that will communicate with GitLab, it will check the permissions you have against your own user account.

One thing to remember is that you can only use one SSH key for one account, as it will be account-bound.

Creating your first Git project

In this recipe, we will take a look at creating your first Git project on your local machine. If you're a Windows user, please make sure that you use Git Bash. This way, you can use the same commands as the ones Linux and OS X users use.

We're going to create a project called `super-git`.

How to do it...

To create our first Git project, perform the following steps:

1. Open your terminal and browse to the folder where you want to create your project.

2. Create a folder named `super-git` and create the following directory inside it:

    ```
    $ mkdir super-git
    $ cd super-git
    ```

3. To make this folder a Git project, we need to tell Git to monitor this folder. We do this by typing the following command:

    ```
    $ git init
    ```

    The following screenshot shows you the output for this command:

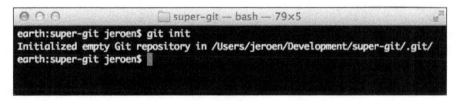

4. Let's create one file to add to the repository. We name it `README.md`:

    ```
    $ echo "HELLO README" > README.md
    ```

5. Now, we will add this new file to Git. This is also known as staging the files:

    ```
    $ git add README.md
    ```

6. Commit the file to our local repository:

```
$ git commit -m "Our first commit"
```

The following screenshot shows you the output of this command:

```
⊖ ○ ○            super-git — bash — 58×5
earth:super-git jeroen$ git commit -m "Our first commit"
[master (root-commit) 95e19fe] Our first commit
 1 file changed, 1 insertion(+)
 create mode 100644 README.md
earth:super-git jeroen$
```

How it works...

We just created our first Git project called `super-git`, created a file, and committed that file to the repository.

Let's go through the steps we took, and I'll explain a little more about what we did.

Every Git project is just a folder that is tracked by Git. This is why we needed to first create a folder where we wanted to store our project. After we created the folder, we ran a `git init` command. This command creates a `.Git` folder with some subdirectories for Git to track your changes. The Git `init` command can be run as many times as you want. It will just create the Git project once.

Next was the creation of a file. As Git does not track empty folders, we had to create a file so that the repository was not empty anymore. Every project benefits from a good `README` file, so this is the first file that we'll create.

Before you can commit a file, you need to tell Git that you want to stage that particular file. Staging a file means that you want Git to commit that file on the next commit. In our case, we just told Git that we wanted to stage one file, but if you have a lot of changes, and want to stage them all, you can stage them using the `git add --all` command.

We had to tell Git to commit the file that we staged to our local repository, and we did this by performing the `git commit -m "your commit message"` command. The `-m` parameter is for the commit message. If you want to enter a longer commit message, you can do so by only typing `git commit`. This will open your editor, and you can change your commit message this way.

Cloning your repository and pushing code to it

In this recipe, we will take a look at cloning your repository from GitLab to your local machine. When you use Git Bash on Windows, the commands will be the same.

Getting ready

You need to create a new repository in your GitLab instance. In this example, we will use the repository named `super-git`.

How to do it...

In the following steps, we will set up our repository and push code to it:

1. Go to the newly created repository.

2. Select the URL in the top-right section.

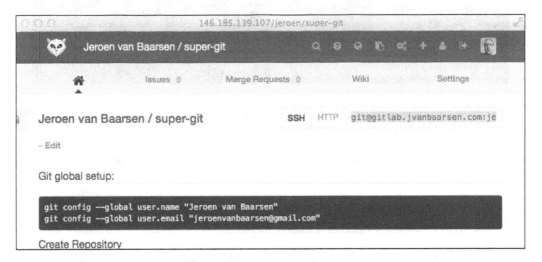

3. Go to the folder where you want to check out the project in the terminal. No need to create a new folder for the project.

4. Enter the Git `clone` command, and change the URL to the URL you just copied:

   ```
   $ git clone URL
   ```

   In my case, the URL is as follows:

   ```
   $ git clone git@146.185.139.107:jeroen/super-git.git
   ```

The following screenshot shows you the output of this command:

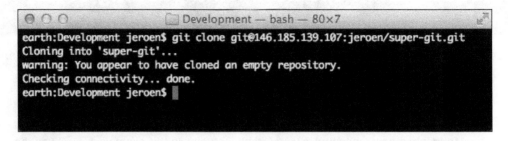

5. You can now go to the folder and check whether it is a Git folder by running the following command:

    ```
    $ git status
    ```

    The following screenshot shows you the output of this command:

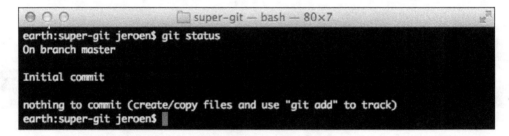

6. Now, we create a change that we can commit:

    ```
    $ echo "Hello GitLab" >> README.md
    ```

7. Next, we add this file to the stage. We can do this by running the following command:

    ```
    $ git add README.md
    ```

8. To commit the change, we run the following command:

    ```
    $ git commit -m "Added readme file"
    ```

9. Now, we have the commit in our local Git repository, but to send it to the GitLab server, we have to enter another command:

    ```
    $ git push -u origin master
    ```

The following screenshot shows you the output of this command:

```
earth:super-git jeroen$ git push origin master
Counting objects: 3, done.
Writing objects: 100% (3/3), 233 bytes | 0 bytes/s, done.
Total 3 (delta 0), reused 0 (delta 0)
To git@146.185.139.107:jeroen/super-git.git
 * [new branch]      master -> master
earth:super-git jeroen$
```

10. When we take a look at our GitLab instance in the following screenshot, we see that the code has been sent here:

How it works...

Git works as a decentralized repository system, which means that there is no central server on which you can store your code. Instead, every user has their own local copy of the entire Git project. If you want to move your code to another server, let's say GitLab, you have to tell GitLab where that server is.

If you have created a new project, you can do this easily by cloning the repository like we just did. However, in case you already have the repository on your local system, you can tell GitLab where the server is by pointing it to the existing GitLab repository.

You can add a new remote by executing the `git remote add NAME URL` command, for example, `git remote add origin git@gitlab.com:example/example.git`.

The remote address is the URL that Git is using to push the code to. It's a convention that uses the origin as the main repository's URL.

When you clone a repository, the name of the remote will be `origin`. So, when we try to push our local commits to the GitLab server, we have to tell it where we want the commits to go. We do this by running `git push -u origin master`. `origin` is the remote server, and `master` is the branch we want to push a commit to.

Working with branches

One of the great powers of Git is the cheapness of creating branches. Branches are a way to create new code away from the central code path. You can see a branch as a tree, and you have a tree branch that sticks out of the tree.

So, when you want to test a new feature, just create a new branch. If you like the feature, you can merge it back. If you don't like the feature, you can remove the branch and no harm is done to the main branch.

In this recipe, we will take a look at how to create branches in Git, where you can find the branches in GitLab, and even how you can create a branch right in the GitLab interface.

Getting ready

You need to have a repository with at least one file, and commit changes in it. In the examples, I'll be using the `super-git` project created at the start of this chapter.

How to do it...

In the following steps, we will use branches to push our code:

1. Go to your Git project in the terminal.

2. Tell Git to create a new branch and decide what name it should have:

   ```
   $ git branch first-branch
   ```

3. At this point, we're not working on the new branch yet. Let's switch to the new branch:

   ```
   $ git checkout first-branch
   ```

   There is a shortcut to have step 2 and 3 combined into one command. It is as follows:

   ```
   $ git checkout -b first-branch
   ```

4. Let's make a change on our newly created branch:

   ```
   echo "Change" >> README.md
   ```

5. Now that we have made a change, let's commit the change:

```
git commit -a -m 'Readme changed'
```

6. We want to have our branch in GitLab, so let's do that now:

```
git push -u origin first-branch
```

The following screenshot shows you the output of this command:

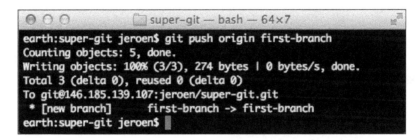

7. Verify that the branch was pushed to our GitLab instance, log in to GitLab, and go to the `super-git` project. You should see text such as `Your name pushed new branch`.

8. Now that we have verified that our branch has been pushed to GitLab, let's take a look at all the branches that this project has. Click on the **branches** text under the SSH URL.

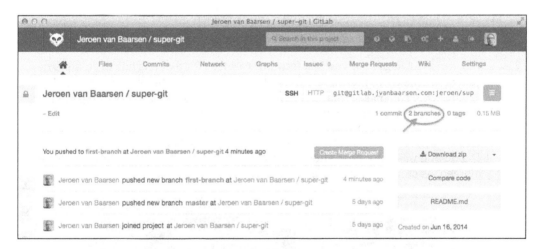

9. You should see a list of two branches: one is named **master** and the other is the branch we just pushed, which is **first-branch**.

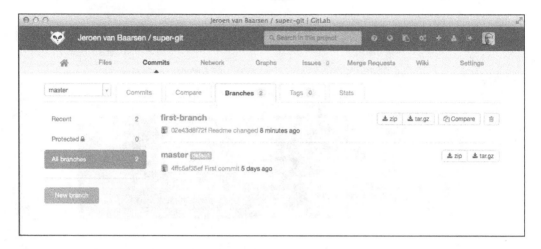

10. Now that we are happy with the changes we made in our separate branch, let's merge the changes back to the main branch, which is also called the `master` branch. To do this, go back to your terminal and check out the `master` branch:

```
git checkout master
```

11. Let's merge `first-branch` into the `master` branch:

```
git merge first-branch --no-ff
```

The `--no-ff` flags mean no fast forward. This tells Git that it is has to create a new commit message for this merge. If you don't tell Git to create this commit, it will try to flatten the commits so that you can't see when a branch has been merged in. It's recommended that you use this flag when merging branches.

12. This will open your editor to give you the opportunity to change the commit message. The default will do for now. After you save and close your editor, the branch will be merged, as shown in the following screenshot:

```
earth:super-git jeroen$ git merge first-branch --no-ff
Merge made by the 'recursive' strategy.
 README.md | 1 +
 1 file changed, 1 insertion(+)
earth:super-git jeroen$
```

13. Now that we have the changes in our local repository, let's push these changes back to GitLab:

    ```
    $ git push origin master
    ```

14. We also want to remove the `first-branch` branch, so we keep our branch list nice and clean:

    ```
    $ git push origin --delete first-branch
    ```

    The following screenshot shows you the output of this command:

    ```
    ⊖ ○ ○              super-git — bash — 64×5
    earth:super-git jeroen$ git push origin --delete first-branch
    To git@146.185.139.107:jeroen/super-git.git
     - [deleted]         first-branch
    earth:super-git jeroen$
    ```

15. You can now go back to GitLab and see that the only branch that is present for this project is the `master` branch.

Performing a rebase operation

When you have a long-running branch, you want to sync up with `master` sometimes. You can do this by merging `master` back into your branch, but Git has a better way of doing this. It's called rebasing. With rebasing, you can replay the commits from the branch over which you want to merge your changes. All this happens without a new commit being created and helps keep your history clean.

How to do it...

To see rebasing in action, we need to have a new branch with some commits and one commit in the `master` branch. Let's do that first:

1. Go to the `super-git` project in your terminal and create a new branch:

    ```
    $ git checkout -b rebase-branch
    ```

2. Create a new file and commit it:

    ```
    $ echo "File content" >> another_file.md
    $ git add .
    $ git commit -m 'Another commit'
    ```

3. Now, switch back to the `master` branch:

    ```
    $ git checkout master
    ```

4. Create a commit in the `master` branch:

```
$ echo "1" >> README.md
$ git add .
$ git commit -m 'Commit in master'
```

5. We also want to have the commit that we have executed in `master` in our `rebase-branch`. To do this, we first need to check out the `rebase-branch` branch:

```
git checkout rebase-branch
```

6. Let's perform the actual rebase:

```
git rebase master
```

The following screenshot shows you the output of this command:

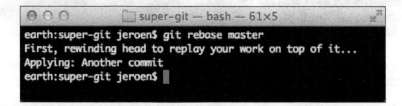

7. Now, you have performed a rebase, but there is a small catch. If you previously pushed your branch to GitLab and performed a rebase, chances are that GitLab will complain if you try to push again. To overcome this issue, you can push the branch with the `-f` flag:

```
git push origin rebase-branch -f
```

Warning! Using the `-f` flag has some dangerous side effects. Make sure that you read the *How it works...* section for more information on this.

How it works...

We just merged the `master` branch into our `rebase-branch` branch without creating a merge commit. This is useful when you work with a larger team, and if everyone just keeps merging everything, you will get a clutter of commit messages.

What a rebase does is takes all the commits that are executed on the branch you want to merge in and replays them over your changes. It will start with the oldest and move all the way to the newest.

At the end, when we tried to push the branch, we had to put the `-f` flag at the end of the `push` command. You want to be careful with that flag as it takes your commit, ignores everything that is remote, and just pushes your changes upstream. The rule of thumb is that you only perform a rebase on a branch that you're working on as a rebase will change history.

Squashing your commits

When you're developing on your machine, chances are that you commit often and every time you commit, your commit message might become a little less explanatory. Commits such as `"Just testing"` or `"lets see if this works"` are common in this phase, which does not make for a nice-looking timeline. Squashing commits makes sure that you have a nice explanatory commit message and that you only have the relevant commits in the Git history.

Before you push all these commits upstream to your GitLab server, you might want to reorder these commits and pack them together in one commit that has a nice commit message and a great explanation of what you've done.

How to do it...

In the following steps, we will squash some commits and push them to the server:

1. Go to the `super-git` project in your terminal.

2. Check out a new branch:

   ```
   $ git checkout -b squash-branch
   ```

3. Let's create two commits in this new branch, which we can squash together:

   ```
   $ echo "1" >> README.md
   $ git add .
   $ git commit -a -m 'wip1'
   $ echo "2" >> README.md
   $ git add .
   $ git commit -a -m 'wip2'
   ```

4. To be sure that we have two commits, let's check the log:

   ```
   $ git log --oneline
   ```

   The following screenshot shows you the output of this command:

   ```
   earth:super-git jeroen$ git log --oneline
   6e5bd08 wip2
   12f904b wip1
   86bf391 Commit in master
   009c172 Merge branch 'first-branch'
   02e43d8 Readme changed
   4ffc5af First commit
   earth:super-git jeroen$
   ```

5. We want the `wip1` and `wip2` commits to be squashed into one commit with a nice commit message. You can do this using the following command:

   $ git rebase -i HEAD~2

   `HEAD~2` means that we want to have the last two commits squashed. If you want to have four commits squashed, the command will end in `HEAD~4`. Keep in mind that at least two commits are required in order to perform a squash operation.

6. Your editor will get opened. You have to change the word `pick` to `squash` in the second line, as shown in the following screenshot:

7. Now, save the file and close the editor.

8. Git will now open another editor window. In this window, you can edit the commit message. Change it to whatever you like.

9. Save the document and close the editor.

10. Git will tell you that the squash was successful.

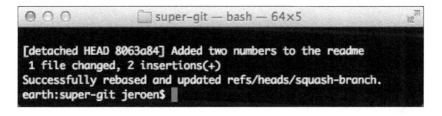

```
super-git — bash — 64×5

[detached HEAD 8063a84] Added two numbers to the readme
 1 file changed, 2 insertions(+)
Successfully rebased and updated refs/heads/squash-branch.
earth:super-git jeroen$
```

11. The last step is to push this branch up to GitLab:

    `git push origin squash-branch`

How it works...

When working on a feature, you want to commit as often as possible, but when you do, most commits won't have the best commit message. Or, when you send out a branch for review, your reviewer might find some points that you need to improve, so another commit will be added to the list.

This list of commits won't look nice in the history, and it won't be easy to revert a change later on. This is where squashing commits comes in. Squashing commits means putting several commits together in one commit, and it even lets you change the commit message.

When the editor was open, we saw a list of the commits we made. They were prefixed with the word `pick`; `pick` means that you want to keep that commit in the history. In the second commit, we replaced the word `pick` with `squash`; this means that we want to squash this commit to the preceding one. When we run a `squash` command, we get the opportunity to change the commit message of the commit we want to squash.

There is another option that might be useful if you don't want to change the commit message, which is the `fixup` command. When you say `fixup`, the commit will be squashed in the preceding commit, but the commit message of the fixed commit will be lost. This is particularly useful if you have a commit that only says `"Just testing"` or something similar.

3
Managing Users, Groups, and Permissions

In this chapter, we will cover the following recipes:

- ▸ Adding a user
- ▸ Creating a group
- ▸ Working with user permissions
- ▸ Protecting your main branches
- ▸ Configuring the project's visibility
- ▸ Removing a user

Introduction

GitLab is based on user interaction, but you want to have some control over all the users in your system. In this chapter, we will take a look at the different types of users that you can add to your project, how you can manage your own groups, and how you can secure your projects from wrongful pushes and prying eyes.

Adding a user

When your team grows, you want to add more users to your system. In this recipe, we take a look at how to invite people to your GitLab system.

How to do it...

At the end of the following points, you will have a new user in your GitLab system:

1. Log in as an admin user.

2. Go to the **Admin area** section.

3. Click on **New User**.

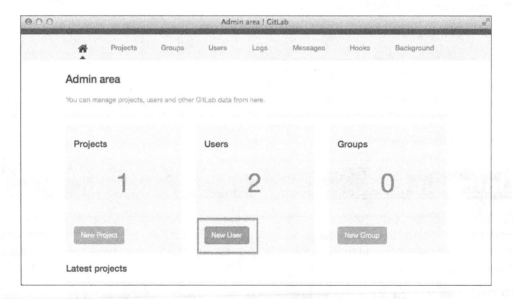

4. Enter the information for the new user. For this example, I'll pick the following information; you can pick whatever you want, but the e-mail address has to be accessible to you as the activation link will be sent there. The following information needs to be given out:

   ❑ **Name**: John Doe

   ❑ **Username**: john.doe

   ❑ **E-mail**: john.doe@example.com

5. Click on **Create User**.

6. Now, check the e-mail address you entered for the user. You should receive an activation e-mail.

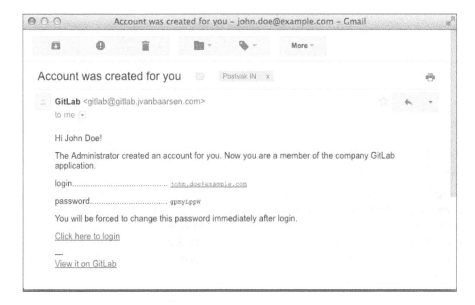

7. Copy the password and click on **Click here to login**.

8. When you log in, you have to pick a new password and click on **Set new password**.

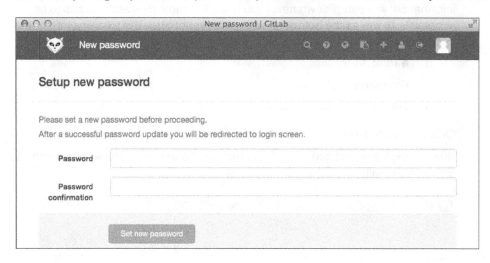

9. You have to log in again with the new password.

You have created a new user!

How it works...

We have just added a new user to GitLab. We entered some basic information, but if you want, you can also add information such as the user's image, Skype name, LinkedIn account, Twitter account, and website. The only thing that you will notice is the avatar, as that is shown in every interaction from this user. Similar to when the user is creating an issue, the avatar will be shown next to the name. The other information will only be shown on the profile page of the given user.

You can also set the project limit for this user; this can be useful if you don't want every user to have a massive amount of private projects. Only projects created by this user will be counted toward the total number. So, when a user is added to a group and the group is creating a project, it will not count the project limit of this user.

We left the **Admin** flag unchecked for this user. This is what you want in most cases as when you check this box, the user will have full control over your GitLab instance as an admin user.

We didn't have to enter a password as GitLab will e-mail the user with a temporary password that the user has to change after the first login.

Creating a group

In this recipe, we will take a look at creating a group. Groups can be used to create a namespace where you put your projects. You can also give people permissions on the group level. When you create a new project, all the group members will automatically have access to that project.

How to do it...

Let's add a group by performing the following steps:

1. Log in as admin.

2. Go to the **Admin area** section.

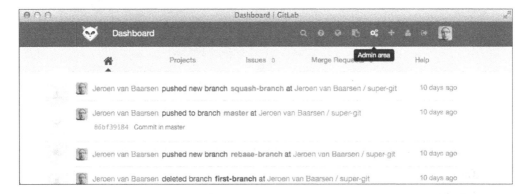

3. Click on **New Group**.

4. Enter a group name and an optional group description and click on **Create Group**.

5. You will be redirected to the new group page.

6. To add a new user, you have to enter their username in the search for a user box.

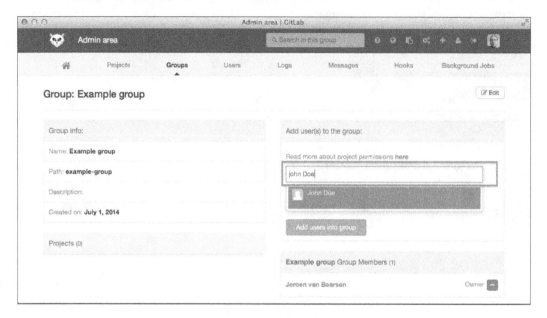

7. In the permission drop-down box, select **Developer**.

8. Click on **Add users into group**.

9. You now see two users in the **Group Members** box.

You have now created a group and added a member to the group.

How it works...

Groups are GitLab's way of introducing namespacing for your projects. So, if your project has multiple repositories, you can create a group for this project and add all the repositories in this group. A benefit you have is that you don't have to add users to every repository separately, but you can just add them to the group and they will automatically be added to the repositories.

After you have created a group, you will automatically be added to the group as **Owner**. For a new user who gets added to the group, you can set five different group access levels: **Guest**, **Reporter**, **Developer**, **Master**, and **Owner**. Only the master and owner access levels have extra permissions in the group; the other permission levels will only apply to the projects created in the group.

The master can create projects in the group, and the owner can also edit and remove the group and manage the group members.

To learn more about permissions, refer to the *Working with User permissions* section in this chapter.

Working with user permissions

You probably don't want every user in your system to be an administrator, or perhaps you have a project where you only want other people to be able to create issues and not commit code. In any of these cases, you need to use the permission model in GitLab. In this recipe, we will take a look at this.

Getting ready

To complete this recipe, you need at least two users in your GitLab instance, one of which needs to be an admin. You also need at least one project; I'll use the `super-git` project from the previous chapter.

How to do it...

Let's see how you can add permissions to your users with the following steps:

1. Go to your project in GitLab.

2. Click on **Settings**.

3. Click on **Members**.
4. Click on **New Project Member**.
5. Type in the name of the user you want to add.

6. In the **Project Access** dropdown, select **Guest**.

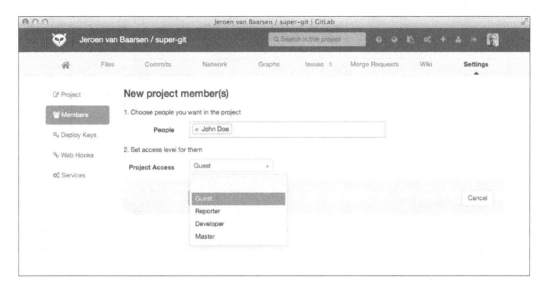

7. Click on **Add Users**.
8. Log out and log in again as the user you have just added.
9. Go to the project you have given this user access to.

    If you take a look at the menu bar in the following screenshot, you can see that this user has significantly fewer items in there. This is because the guest user can only view the project issues.

You have just added a user to your project and given him certain permissions.

How it works...

In GitLab, you can protect your project with user permissions. There are five different permissions: **Guest**, **Reporter**, **Developer**, **Master**, and **Owner**. The **Owner** permission is not a permission that you can grant someone. The creator of a project will automatically have this permission.

Let's put the permissions in a table for a nice overview:

	Guest	Reporter	Developer	Master	Owner
Create new issues	*	*	*	*	*
Leave comments	*	*	*	*	*
Pull the project code		*	*	*	*
Download a project		*	*	*	*
Create code snippets		*	*	*	*
Create new merge requests			*	*	*
Push changes to nonprotected branches			*	*	*
Remove nonprotected branches			*	*	*
Add tags			*	*	*
Write a wiki			*	*	*
Manage the issue tracker			*	*	*
Add new team members				*	*
Push changes to protected branches				*	*
Manage the branch protection				*	*
Manage Git tags				*	*
Edit the project				*	*
Add deploy keys to the project				*	*
Configure the project hooks				*	*

The different permission models are really useful in cases where you have a senior developer who you want to give access to everything. However, if you hire an intern, this intern should only have access to pulling code and not deleting branches and stuff. This way, you can make sure that the senior developer has reviewed the code before it was merged into the main branch.

Protecting your main branches

You might want to protect your most important branches against directly pushing changes to them, or more importantly protect them against force pushing, which is pushing to your repository without taking changes by other people into account, using the -f flag.

Protecting a branch can be done in GitLab by marking a branch as **Protected**. This means that people with the **Developer** permission level and lower are not able to push changes directly to that branch; they need to create a merge request to push changes to these branches. Also, this prevents anyone from force pushing to that branch.

How to do it...

In the following steps, we will protect a branch:

1. Log in to your GitLab instance as an admin.
2. Go to the project you want to protect.
3. Click on **Settings**.

4. Click on **Protected branches**.

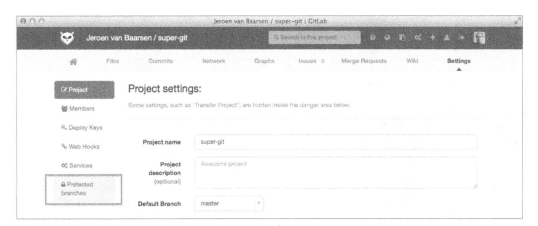

5. In the dropdown, select the branch you want to protect and click on **Protect**.

6. You will now see a list of your protected branches.

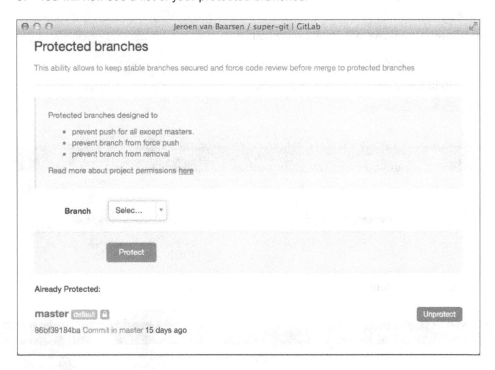

How it works...

Some branches are crucial to your workflow. Think about the **Master** branch, the **Acceptance** branch, or the **Production** branch. You don't want people to directly commit to them or force push to these branches. This is where protecting your branches comes in.

One other nice thing about the protected branches is that you're secure from accidental branch deletions as GitLab will block every attempt to delete this branch as long as it is marked protected.

Configuring the project's visibility

GitLab allows you to have three types of projects: **Private**, **Internal**, and **Public**. In this recipe, we are going to change the `super-git` project we created in the previous chapter from a private project to a public project.

When you have a public project, people will be able to view that project even when they don't have an account on your system. People without an account are able to pull the code; people who have an account on your GitLab server but don't have direct access to the project are able to create merge requests and open issues.

How to do it...

In the following steps, we will configure the project's visibility:

1. Log in to your GitLab instance as a project owner.
2. Select the project for which you want to change the visibility.
3. Click on **Settings**.

4. Select **Public** in the **Visibility Level** section.

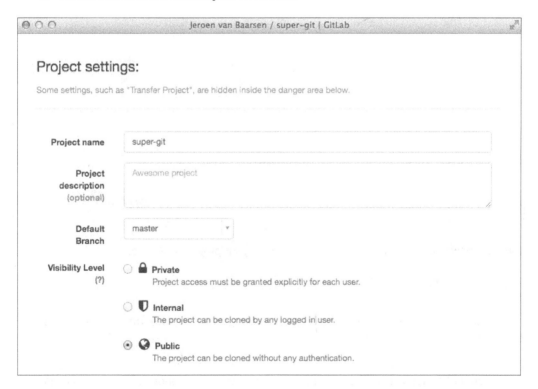

5. Click on **Save changes**.

6. At this point, you have made your project public. Let's take a look to confirm this.

7. Log out as the current user.

8. Select **public projects** in the login screen.

9. On this page, you see all the public projects in your GitLab instance.

You have now successfully changed the visibility of your project to **Public**.

How it works...

In GitLab, you can have three different project visibility levels: **Private**, **Internal**, and **Public**. The default is **Private**.

Private projects mean that they are only visible to the users you've added to your projects. The amount of options an invited person in your project has depends on the permissions you grant them.

If you want to have a project that is accessible to all users who have an account on your GitLab instance, you can select the **Internal** visibility level. Any logged in user will have guest permissions to the project.

The last visibility option you can set is **Public**; this is the one we used in this recipe. A public project can be cloned without any authentication. The public projects will also be listed on the public access directory.

You can restrict the use of public or internal projects by changing the `gitlab.yml` file. This way, you can disable the option for people to create public or internal projects for the entire GitLab installation.

Removing a user

At some point in the lifetime of your GitLab instance, you need to remove a user. GitLab offers two ways of doing this: one is completely removing a user from the system and the other one is just blocking the user so that they can't log in anymore.

Getting ready

To complete this recipe, you need to have at least two users: a user who has administrator privileges and a user for whom we can block access.

How to do it...

In the following steps, we will block a user from your GitLab server:

1. Log in as a user with administrator permissions.
2. Go to the **Admin area** section.

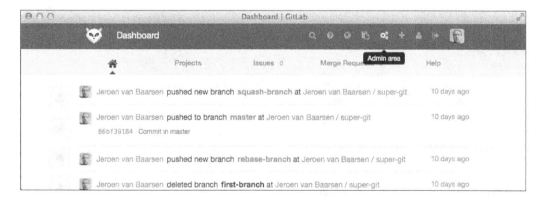

3. Click on **Users**.

4. Click on **Block** for the user that you want to block.

5. You need to confirm that you want to block this user.

6. After you have blocked the user, it will be removed from the list and will be moved to the **Blocked** users list.

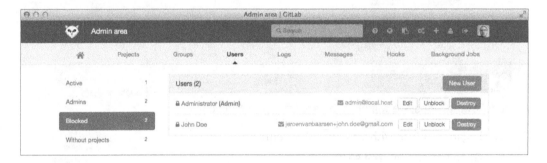

You have successfully blocked the user.

How it works...

When you want to remove a user from your system, you have to make a decision: does this user have a lot of projects and issues created or not? The reason this is a key decision is because when you completely remove a user from the system, all of its dependencies are deleted as well. What does that mean? Well, if you have a user who has 10 issues created and you delete that particular user, all the 10 issues will be deleted as well. For this reason, I recommend that you block a user instead of deleting them.

A blocked user can't log in to the system, but all of the user's dependencies remain in your system. When a blocked user tries to log in to the system, they will see a message stating **Your account is blocked. Retry when an admin has unblocked it**.

4
Issue Tracker and Wiki

In this chapter, we will cover the following recipes:

- ► Creating your first issue
- ► Creating your first merge request
- ► Accepting a merge request
- ► Working with milestones
- ► Referencing issues in commits
- ► Creating your first wiki page
- ► Managing the wiki with Gollum

Creating your first issue

When working on projects, you get bugs or new feature requests. You need a place to store all of them. GitLab has an amazing and easy way to do this; it's called the issue tracker. In this recipe, we will take a look at how you can create these issues in the issue tracker.

With the issue tracker, you can assign issues to team members and follow the path of a bug from it being reported to it being solved. When you work in a team, it's very useful to know who is working on what so that you don't work on the same thing without knowing. Here, the assignment of issues comes in. When you start working on an issue, or when you create the issue and already know who is going to work on it, you can assign the issue to that person.

Getting ready

You need to have one project in your GitLab server; I'll be using the `super-git` project that we created in a previous chapter.

How to do it...

Let's create an issue with the following steps:

1. Log in to your GitLab instance.

2. Go to your project.

3. Click on **Issues**.

4. Now, you can see the issue overview. Click on the **New Issue** button.

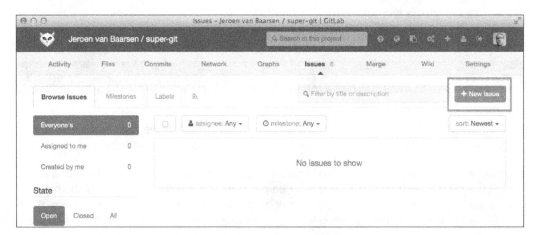

5. You then see a form that is required to create an issue. Let's fill it in.

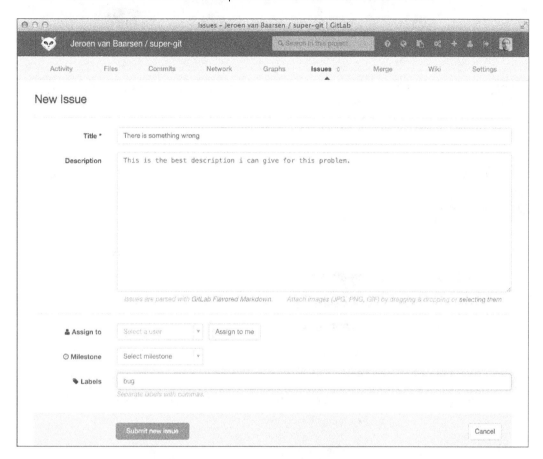

6. Click on **Submit new issue**.

7. You will be redirected to that issue; this is where you can discuss the issue.

How it works...

We have just created a basic issue with nothing more than a title and a small description of the issue. However, there is more that you can do.

In some cases, when you want to report a UI bug, for example, you want to be able to add some screenshot of the problem so that the next person who comes in and takes the issue has a good understanding of the issue. GitLab makes this super easy; just drag the image into the text area, and it will automatically upload the file and create the markdown-formatted text for the image.

Creating your first merge request

When you're done editing code, you might want your peers to review it. Instead of mailing patches around, you can do this in a super easy way in GitLab using a merge request.

A merge request is like an issue, but it has the diff of the code change attached to it, and users can create line-by-line comments on the code.

Getting ready

To follow this recipe, you need a project in GitLab, and you need that project cloned to your local system so that you can edit some code. I'll be using the `super-git` project we created in a previous chapter.

How to do it...

Perform the following steps to create a merge request:

1. Go to the project on your local machine:

   ```
   cd ~/Development/super-git/
   ```

2. Make sure you're on the `master` branch:

   ```
   git checkout master
   ```

3. Before we make any changes to the code, we want to create a new `feature` branch:

   ```
   git checkout -b awesome-feature
   ```

4. Let's make a change to the `README.md` file:

   ```
   echo "Change" >> README.md
   ```

5. Now, we will commit this change:

   ```
   git commit -a -m 'Added text to readme'
   ```

6. Push the `feature` branch to GitLab:

   ```
   git push origin awesome-feature
   ```

7. Go to your GitLab instance and log in.

8. On the dashboard, a message will indicate that you just pushed a branch, as shown in the following screenshot. Next to this message, GitLab offers the option to create a merge request from this branch. This can be a useful shortcut in order to avoid filling out the **New Merge Request** form.

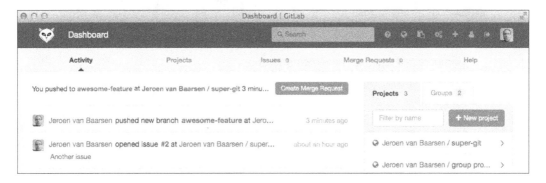

9. As this option only shows the latest pushed branch, it's also valuable to know where you can create a merge request manually. Let's do that for this merge request.

10. Go to your project.

11. Click on **Merge Requests**.

12. Click on the **New Merge Request** option.

13. You will see a form where you have to select the branch for which you want to create a merge request. Select the branch you just pushed, that is, **awesome-feature**.

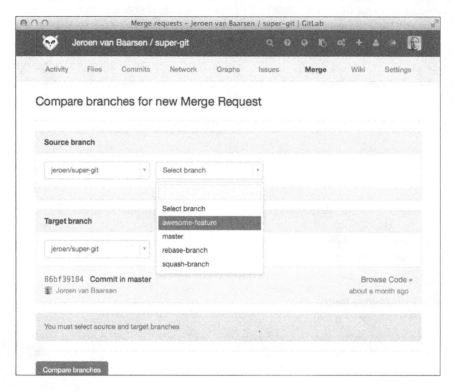

14. Click on **Compare branches**.

15. Fill in the form shown in the following screenshot with some useful information about the change we just made:

16. Click on **Submit merge request**.

17. Your merge request is now created, and you will be redirected to the merge request page.

How it works...

When working on new code, it's useful to have a peer review the code before it gets merged into the `master` branch. Merge requests are a great way to have another person review your code.

When creating a merge request, you first have to select which branch you want to merge and what the target branch will be. GitLab has automatically selected the default branch for you and where you want to merge it to. The only thing left for you is to select what branch you want to merge.

After you have selected what you want to merge to, you need to fill in a little form; this is to explain what you have changed, and it also explains why you have changed this part of code. A good template that can be used when creating a merge request is the following:

- ▶ What does this merge request do?
- ▶ Are there any points the reviewer has to double-check?
- ▶ Why was this merge request needed?
- ▶ What are the relevant issue numbers?
- ▶ Screenshots (if appropriate)

This way, every merge request has the same textual setup, and it's easier to scan them.

If you want, you can assign the merge request to a specific person in the team, just like an issue.

Accepting a merge request

Once a person in your team has created a merge request, you have to review it, possibly leave some comments, and, at last, merge the merge request. This recipe will help guide you through this process.

Getting ready

Before you can start this recipe, you will need a repository with at least one merge request. If you followed the *Creating your first merge request* recipe, you can use that one.

How to do it...

In the following steps, we will accept a merge request:

1. Log in to your GitLab instance.
2. Go to the project for which the merge request has been made, in our case, the `super-git` project.

3. Click on **Merge Requests**:

4. You now see an overview with all the merge requests created for this project. Click on the **Awesome feature** merge request.

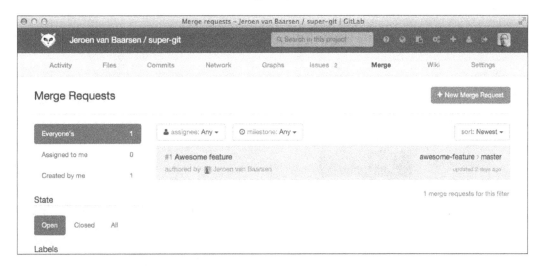

5. You're now viewing the actual merge request. This is also the place where you will have the discussion on this feature. You can take a look at the actual code changes in the **Changes** section.

6.   For now, this code change looks good! Let's merge this. At the top, you see a box with the **You can accept this request automatically.** text. Don't forget to also click on the **Remove source-branch** checkbox, and click on **Accept Merge Request**.

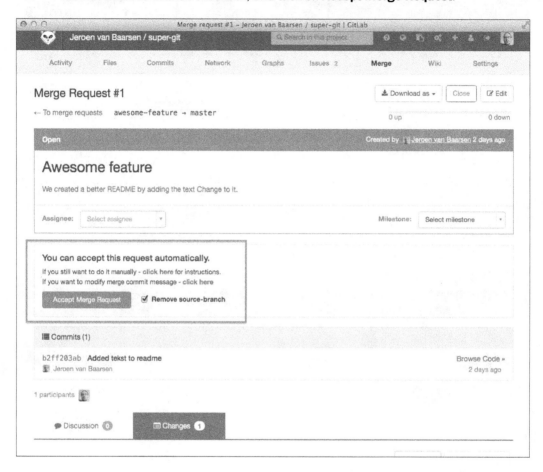

7. GitLab will be busy for a little while, and eventually, the page will refresh. It will now say that the merge request has been merged:

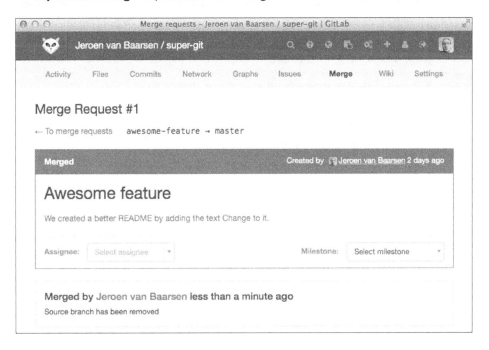

How it works...

Once a person has created a merge request and assigned you as the assignee, you get an e-mail saying that a new merge request has been created. You can then start reviewing the code when you see something that you think can be done better, or maybe, you just want to compliment someone on an awesome piece of code; you can do so by selecting the line, and a comment box will appear. Here, you can type in your comment. Once you create the comment, the person who has created the merge request will get an e-mail.

Every time a new commit gets added to the branch that is used for the merge request, it will be automatically added to the merge request; this keeps reviewing easy!

Once the code that you've commented on has changed, it will say that you've commented on an out-of-date piece of code.

When a merge request is open for a little while, it can happen that it is not ready to be merged anymore because of conflicts. Instead of opening a new merge request, the author can rebase with the conflicting branch and push back to GitLab; this will make the merge request mergeable again.

Referencing issues

You have created an issue in GitLab and are about to commit the code that solves a specific problem. You want to be able to reference that specific issue from your commit message, or even better, close that issue once the commit has been merged! In this recipe, we will take a look at the possibility of referencing issues and merge requests from your commits.

How to do it...

In the following steps, we will see how referencing works:

1. Log in to GitLab.
2. Go to the super-git project.
3. Create an issue in that project.
4. To reference the issue in our commit messages, we must know the issue number. You can find it in the issue overview.

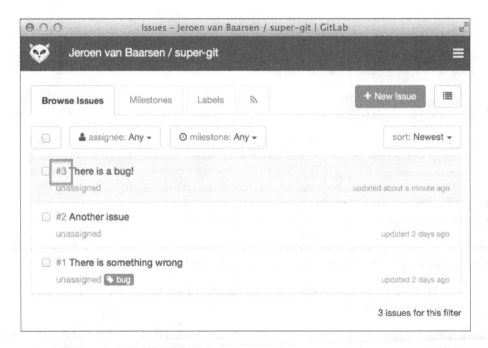

5. Now, create a commit that will close this issue. To do this, go to the cloned project on our local machine.

6. Before we make the actual change, make sure that your local repository is up to date:

```
git checkout master && git pull
```

7. Now, create a feature branch in which we make this change:

```
git checkout -b bug-fix
```

8. Make the change that will fix this nasty bug:

```
echo "Lets fix this bug" >> README.md
```

9. Commit this change and enter the commit message shown in the following screenshot:

```
git commit -a
```

The output of this command is shown in the following screenshot:

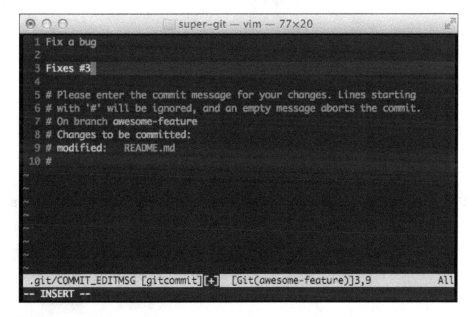

10. Push this commit to GitLab:

```
git push origin bug-fix
```

11. Go to your GitLab instance and create a new merge request for this branch.

12. When you've created the merge request, you will be redirected to the merge request page. You will see a notice that if you accept this merge request, then you will also close issue number 3.

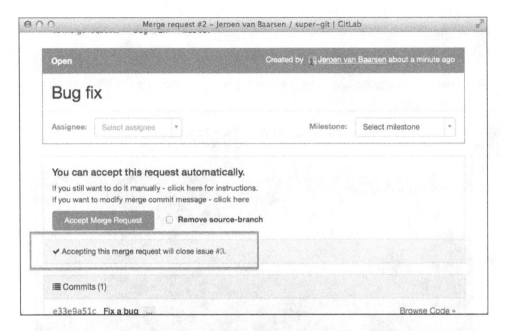

13. Let's merge this merge request and take a look at issue number 3. You have to select the **Closed** tab in the issue overview, otherwise you can't see that specific issue.

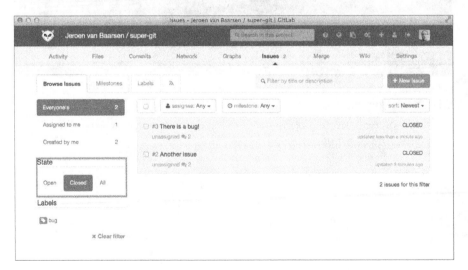

14. Click on the **There is a bug!** issue. You will see a big red border; this tells you that the issue has been closed. Also, there is a comment that says this issue has been closed by a specific commit.

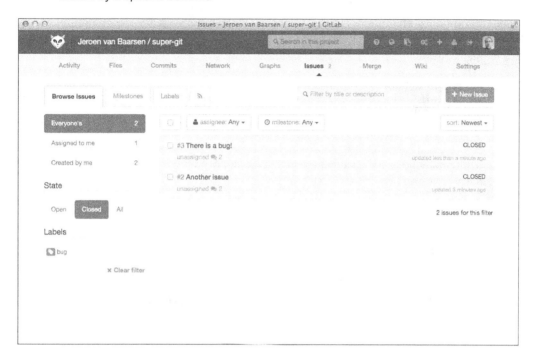

There's more...

GitLab has multiple mention systems in place. The one we have just looked at is for referencing issues. This can not only be done via commits, but you can also mention issues from a merge request or even from another issue.

The other mention methods are:

- ▸ `@user_name`: This mentions a team member.
- ▸ `@all`: This mentions all the team members.
- ▸ `#123`: This mentions a specific issue.
- ▸ `!123`: This mentions a merge request.
- ▸ `$123`: This provides a link to a snippet.
- ▸ `b23cf08`: This provides a link to a specific commit through its `SHA1` hash.
- ▸ `[file](path/to/file)`: This is the link to a file. The file has to be uploaded. This works in the same way as creating a link in Markdown.

Every time you reference a user, that user gets an e-mail saying that he or she got mentioned. This is particularly useful when you are working with a large group of people and want to get someone involved.

When you reference an issue or a merge request, GitLab will create a comment in that specific issue or merge request, saying it got referenced. This is useful when you want to link issues and merge requests together.

Working with milestones

When a project gets a little bigger, it's nice to have some sort of project management system. GitLab can help you with this. We already looked at the issue tracker and merge requests, but we can combine these two in milestones. In this recipe, we will take a look at how you can create milestones and how you can use them most effectively.

How to do it...

Let's create a milestone by performing the following steps:

1. Log in to your GitLab instance.
2. Go to the super-git project or any project you want to create a milestone for.
3. Click on the **Issues** menu item.
4. Click on the **Milestones** tab.

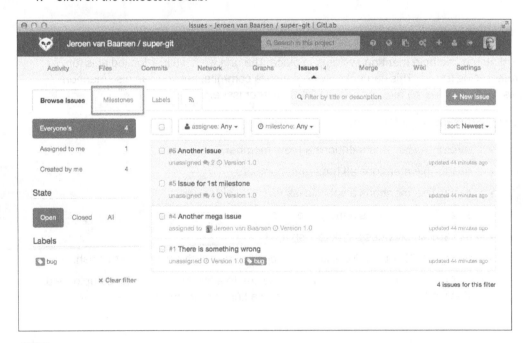

5. Click on **New Milestone**.

6. In the form, fill in the title and an optional due date and description, and click on **Create milestone**.

7. Once the milestone is created, you'll be redirected to the detail view of this milestone. Here, we can add issues for this particular milestone. Let's create two or three issues by clicking on the **New Issue** button.

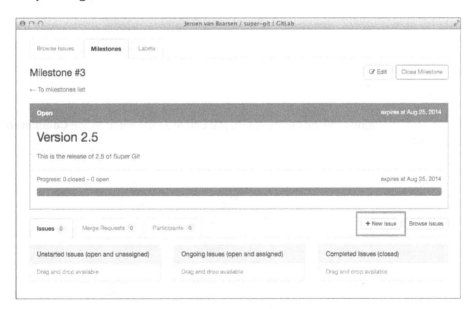

8. To add an issue to this milestone, all you have to do is set the milestone drop-down box to the correct milestone. In our case, set it to **Version 2.5**.

9. Now, we have created a few issues. We can see the issue flow in a milestone in a slightly better manner. Let's take an issue and drop it in the **Ongoing Issues** list.

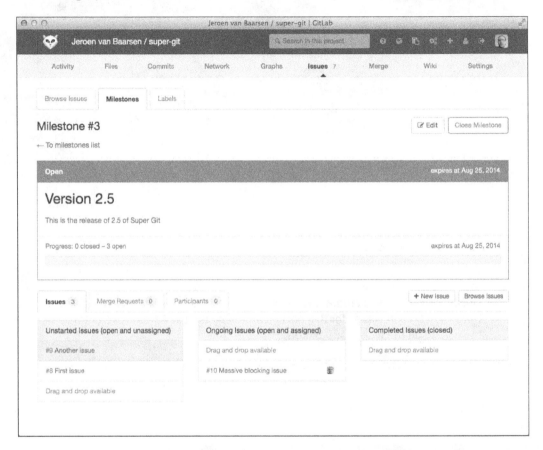

10. When you're done working on the issue, you can drag the issue to the **Completed Issues** list.

11. Once you've done that, let's go to the issue we've just closed. As you can see, GitLab automatically adds comments to the issue whenever something has changed on the milestone board.

How it works...

When you're planning a new version or maybe just a big feature, it's nice to see a quick overview of the status of the work and have all the issues and merge requests grouped together.

GitLab's answer to this is milestones. With milestones, you have a bird's-eye overview of the project. You can see what status an issue has, who is working on it, and also a quick overview of all the merge requests and their status.

You can use the milestones for a project that has an end date, but you can also use them for ongoing projects. For example, you're running a project and you want a place where you can store all the bugs so that you have a quick overview of all the bugs that exist, but you don't want to be bothered by issues about new features. In this case, you can create a milestone named Bugs, and if you don't give it a deadline, it will stay open until you close the milestone manually.

Creating your first wiki page

GitLab offers a nice way to keep information and knowledge for a project in the project. You can use the well-known format of a wiki for this. In this recipe, we will take a look at how to create wiki pages in GitLab from the web interface.

How to do it...

In the following steps, we will create a wiki page:

1. Log in to your GitLab instance.
2. Go to the project for which you want to create a wiki.
3. Click on the **Wiki** menu item.

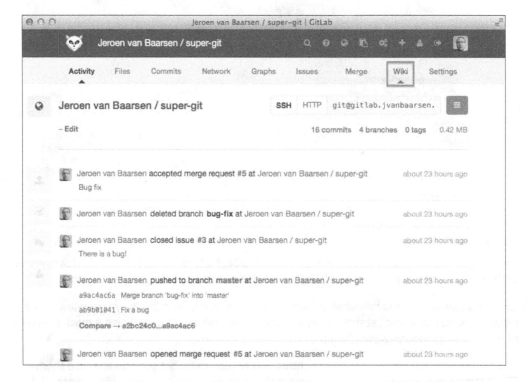

4. Click on the **New Page** button.
5. In the pop up, enter the name of the page; you can't use spaces in the name. Let's pick the name **awesome-wiki**.

6. When you click on the **Build** button, you will be redirected to the newly created wiki page. Here, you can add some content. After you're done adding content, you need to enter a commit message. For now, let's enter `created first wiki page`.

7. Now, click on **Create Page**, and your wiki page will be created.

How it works...

The simplest way to create a wiki page in GitLab is by adding pages through the web interface. You get a view where you can enter the content, add a commit message, and create the wiki page.

The pages are not stored in the database, though. GitLab uses Gollum under the hood, so all your wiki pages are stored in a Git repository. This repository gets created when you create a project, and you can choose whether you want to have a wiki as well.

The repository that gets created has the following URL format:

```
git@example.com:namespace/projectname.wiki.git
```

Managing your wiki with Gollum

The wiki in GitLab can be managed via the web interface, but it is also possible to edit it locally using the Gollum gem. In this recipe, we will take a look at what is needed to get the wiki running on your local machine, make a change, and push it back to GitLab.

Getting ready

To follow this recipe, you need to have Ruby installed on your system, and you need the permissions to install new gems on your machine. Also, you need to have a project in GitLab that has at least one wiki page.

How to do it...

Let's create a wiki article using Gollum with the following steps:

1. Install Gollum on your local machine. This might take a while:

   gem install gollum

2. Now, clone the wiki. You can find the Git URL in the top-right section on the wiki page of your project.

3. You can clone the project just like any other Git project.

4. Go to the folder you just cloned.

5. Enter the `gollum` command. This will start the Gollum server so that you can watch your changes in your browser.

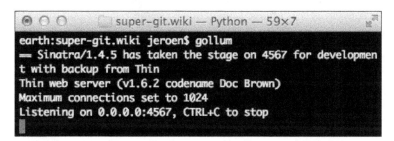

6. When you go to `localhost:4567` in your browser, you'll see a text editor where you can edit your wiki.

7. Create a new page, and click on the **New** button.

8. You need to enter a page name. Let's name it `about-git` and click on **OK**.

9. Fill in the form. Once you're done, click on **Save**.

10. To push these changes back to GitLab, all we have to do is execute a Git push on the terminal. Close the Gollum server, and push the changes to GitLab:

    `git push`

11. Go to your GitLab instance, and take a look at the wiki.

12. Select the **Pages** tab on the wiki page.

13. You can now see the newly created wiki pages on GitLab!

How it works...

Besides managing the wiki via the GitLab interface, you can also check out the project to your local machine and manage the wiki that way. The benefit of this approach is that you always have a copy of all your wiki information on your local machine. So, if you don't have a working Internet connection, you're still able to find all the important information about the project you're working on.

One of the downsides of running the wiki on your local machine is that you need to have some dependencies installed; one of these dependencies is a Ruby installation. If you're running Mac OS X, you're good to go, as this OS gets shipped with a working Ruby.

If you're on a Windows system, you need to install Ruby yourself.

Another dependency that you need to have installed is the Gollum gem. This installs the system that will eventually run the wiki on your local machine, so you can view the pages. This is done by running `bundle install gollum` on your terminal.

5
Maintaining Your GitLab Instance

In this chapter, we will cover the following recipes:

- ▶ Updating an Omnibus installation
- ▶ Updating GitLab from a source installation
- ▶ Troubleshooting your GitLab installation
- ▶ Creating a backup
- ▶ Restoring a backup
- ▶ Importing Git repositories

Introduction

When running your GitLab installation, you need to update it every once in a while. GitLab is released every 22nd day of the month, so around the end of the month would be a nice time to update! The releases on the 22nd day are well tested, as `gitlab.com` is using the release candidates in production all the time. This way, you can be sure that the release meets the standards of the GitLab team!

In this chapter, we will take a look at how you can update your GitLab server and how you can create backups and restore them.

If you want to know what has changed in the new release, you can take a look at the change log provided in the repository for GitLab at `https://gitlab.com/gitlab-org/gitlab-ce/blob/master/CHANGELOG`.

Updating an Omnibus installation

In this recipe, we will take a look at how you can update your GitLab installation when you install it via the Omnibus package. In this recipe, I'll make the assumption that you're using Ubuntu 12.04. You can use other Linux distributions; the steps for these can be found at `about.gitlab.com`.

How to do it...

Let's update the Omnibus installation with the following steps:

1. Log in to your server via SSH.

2. Stop the `unicorn` server:

   ```
   $ sudo gitlab-ctl stop unicorn
   ```

3. Stop the background job server:

   ```
   $ sudo gitlab-ctl stop sidekiq
   ```

4. Create a backup in case the upgrade fails:

   ```
   $ sudo gitlab-rake gitlab:backup:create
   ```

5. Download the package from the GitLab website (`https://about.gitlab.com/downloads/`):

   ```
   $ wget https://downloads-packages.s3.amazonaws.com/ubuntu-12.04/gitlab_7.1.1-omnibus.1-1_amd64.deb
   ```

6. Install the new package (change the `x.x.x` part to the correct version number from your download):

   ```
   sudo dpkg -i gitlab_x.x.x-omnibus.xxx.deb
   ```

7. Reconfigure GitLab:

   ```
   sudo gitlab-ctl reconfigure
   ```

8. Restart all the services:

   ```
   sudo gitlab-ctl restart
   ```

How it works...

On the 22nd day of every month, a new version of GitLab is released. This also includes the Omnibus package. As the installation of Omnibus based on GitLab does not take very long, the GitLab team has decided to install a new version of GitLab and preserve the old data of the old installation; this way, you don't go over an update process, but you will be guided through the installation process as if you're installing a new GitLab instance.

So, when you're updating an Omnibus-based installation, you're not really updating but rather installing a newer version and reconfiguring it to use the old data.

One thing you have to keep in mind is that making backups is very important. As any update can go wrong at some level, it's a good feeling to know that when stuff goes wrong, you always have a backup that you can use to get back up and running as quickly as possible.

Updating GitLab from a source installation

Updating used to be a lot of work; you had to open the update document to find out that you need to perform about 15 steps to upgrade your GitLab installation.

To tackle this issue, the GitLab team has created a semiautomatic upgrader. When you run the upgrader, it will check whether there is a new minor version. If there is, it will start the upgrade process for you. It will perform database migrations and update config files for you.

How to do it...

Upgrade your source installation with the following steps:

1. Log in to your server using SSH.
2. We start with creating a backup just in case something goes wrong.
3. Go to the folder of your GitLab instance:

   ```
   $ cd /home/git/gitlab
   ```

4. Create the backup; this might take a little while depending on the amount of repositories and the size of each individual repository:

   ```
   $ sudo -u git -H bundle exec rake gitlab:backup:create
   RAILS_ENV=production
   ```

5. Stop the server:

   ```
   $ sudo service gitlab stop
   ```

6. Run the upgrader:

   ```
   $ if [ -f bin/upgrade.rb ]; then sudo -u git -H ruby
   bin/upgrade.rb; else sudo -u git -H ruby script/upgrade.rb; fi
   ```

7. Start the application:

   ```
   $ sudo service gitlab start && sudo service nginx restart
   ```

8. Check whether everything went fine. We can use the self-check GitLab ships with:

   ```
   $ sudo -u git -H bundle exec rake gitlab:check
   RAILS_ENV=production
   ```

9. If the GitLab check indicates that we need to upgrade the GitLab shell, we can do this by performing the following steps.

10. Go to the shell directory:

```
$ cd /home/git/gitlab-shell
```

11. Fetch the latest code:

```
$ sudo -u git -H git fetch
```

12. Run the following command to set the pointer to the latest shell release. Change 1.9.4 to the current version number. You can find this number in the output of the check we did in step 9:

```
sudo -u git -H git checkout v1.9.4
```

How it works...

It is highly recommended that you create a backup before you run the upgrader as every update can break something in your installation. It's a good feeling to know that when all goes wrong, you're prepared and can roll back the upgrade using the backup.

Troubleshooting your GitLab installation

When your GitLab instance does not work the way you expect it to work, it's nice to have a way to check what parts of your installation are not working properly. In this recipe, we will take a look at the self-diagnostic tools provided by GitLab.

How to do it...

Learn how to troubleshoot your GitLab server with the following steps:

1. Log in to your server using SSH.

   The first case shows troubleshooting in the case of a GitLab source installation.

2. Go to your gitlab folder:

```
$ cd /home/git/gitlab
```

3. To autodiagnose your installation, run the following command:

```
$ sudo -u git -H bundle exec rake gitlab:check
RAILS_ENV=production
```

4. When there is a problem with your GitLab installation, it will be outputted in red text, as shown in the following screenshot:

```
 ○ ○ ○                          1. root@gitlab: ~ (ssh)
Projects have satellites? ...
Jeroen van Baarsen / super-git ... yes
Example group / group project ... no
  Try fixing it:
  sudo -u git -H bundle exec rake gitlab:satellites:create RAILS_ENV=production
  If necessary, remove the tmp/repo_satellites directory ...
  ... and rerun the above command
  For more information see:
  doc/raketasks/maintenance.md
  Please fix the error above and rerun the checks.
Jeroen van Baarsen / group project ... yes
Redis version >= 2.0.0? ... yes
Your git bin path is "/opt/gitlab/embedded/bin/git"
Git version >= 1.7.10 ? ... yes (2.0.0)

Checking GitLab ... Finished

root@gitlab:~#
```

5. The solution for the problem is also given; just follow the explanation given by the problem you walk into. In this case, we have to run the following command:

```
$ sudo-u git -h bundle exec rake  gitlab:satellites:create
RAILS_ENV=production
```

6. If everything is green, your installation is in great shape!

   The next few steps concentrate on troubleshooting in the case of the Gitlab Omnibus installation.

7. Run the following command:

```
$ sudo gitlab-rake gitlab:check
```

8. When you have any problem with your GitLab installation, this will be outputted; also, the possible solution will be shown.

9. The solution that is given for this problem is the solution for the source installation. To fix this issue in the Omnibus installation, we need to alter the command a little. You have to replace the `$ sudo-u git -h bundle exec rake` part with `$ sudo gitlab-rake`. So, the command will look as follows:

```
$ sudo gitlab-rake gitlab:satellites:create
RAILS_ENV=production
```

10. If everything is green, your installation is in top shape!

11. In case you need to view the logs, you can run the following command:

```
$ sudo gitlab-ctl tail
```

12. To exit the log flow, use *Ctrl + C*.

How it works...

When you think your GitLab installation might not be in a good shape or you think you've found a bug, it's always a good idea to run the self-diagnostics for GitLab. It will tell you whether you've configured GitLab correctly and whether everything is still up to date.

Here is a list of what will be checked:

- Is your database config correct?
- If your database is still running SQLite instead of PostgreSQL or MySQL, it will give you a warning.
- Are all the user groups configured correctly?
- Is the GitLab config present and up to date?
- Are the logs writable?
- Is the `tmp` directory writable?
- Is the `init` script present and up to date?
- Are all the projects namespaced? This is important if you've upgraded from an old version.
- Are all the satellites present?
- Is your Redis up to date?
- Is the correct Ruby version being used?
- Is the correct Git version being used?

This is the first place you should start when walking into problems. If this does not give you the correct answers, you can open an issue on the GitLab repository (`https://gitlab.com/gitlab-org/gitlab-ce`). Make sure you post the output of this check as well, as you will most likely be asked to post it anyway.

Creating a backup

It's important that you have your source code secured so that when your laptop breaks down—or even worse, the office got destroyed—the most valuable part of your company (besides the employees, of course) is still intact. You've already taken an important step into the right direction; you set up a Git server so that your source code has multiple places to live. However, what if that server breaks down?

This is where backups come into play! GitLab Omnibus makes it really easy to create backups. With just a simple command, everything in your system gets backed up: the repositories as well as the databases. It's all packed in a tar ball, so you can store it elsewhere, for example, Amazon S3 or just another server somewhere else.

In this recipe, we not only created a backup, but also created a schema to automatically back up the creation using crontabs. This way, you can rest assured that all of your code gets backed up every night.

How to do it...

In the following steps, we will set up the backups for GitLab:

1. First, log in to your server using SSH.

    The first few steps concentrate on the GitLab source installation.

2. Go to your gitlab folder:

    cd /home/git/gitlab

3. Run the backup command:

    bundle exec rake gitlab:backup:create RAILS_ENV=production

    The backup will now run. This might take a while depending on the number of repositories and the size of each repository.

    The backups will be stored in the /home/git/gitlab/tmp/backups directory.

    Having to create a backup by hand everyday is no fun, so let's automate the creation of backups using a cronjob file.

4. Run the following command to open the cronjob file:

    $ sudo -u git crontab -e

5. Add the following content to the end of the file:

    ```
    0 2 * * * cd /home/git/gitlab &&
    PATH=/usr/local/bin:/usr/bin:/bin bundle exec rake
        gitlab:backup:create RAILS_ENV=production
    ```

6. Save the file, and the backups will be created everyday at 2 A.M.

    The next few steps talk about the GitLab Omnibus installation.

7. To create the backup, run the following command:

    $ sudo gitlab-rake gitlab:backup:create

    A backup is now created in the $ /var/opt/gitlab/backups directory.

8. Let's verify that our backup is actually there:

    ```
    $ ls /var/opt/gitlab/backups/
    ```

    You should see at least one filename, such as `1404647816_gitlab_backup.tar`. The number in the filename is a timestamp, so this might differ in your case.

    Now we know how to create the backup. Let's automate this via a `cronjob` file.

9. Run the following command as the root user:

    ```
    $ crontab -e
    ```

10. Add the following code to the end of the file to have the backup run every day at 2 A.M.:

    ```
    0 2 * * * /opt/gitlab/bin/gitlab-rake gitlab:backup:create
    ```

    After you save the file, a backup will be created every day at 2 A.M. This is great, but there is a tiny catch; if you have the backups run for too long, it will take up all of your disk space. Let's fix this!

11. Open this file location: `/etc/gitlab/gitlab.rb`.

12. Let's have the backups only last for a week. After that, they will be destroyed. 7 days is 604,800 seconds. Add the following code to the bottom of the file:

    ```
    gitlab_rails['backup_keep_time'] = 604800
    ```

13. To have the changes take effect, we have to tell GitLab to reconfigure itself. Run the following command:

    ```
    $ sudo gitlab-ctl reconfigure
    ```

Restoring a backup

If your server breaks down, it is nice to have a backup. However, it's a pain when it's a full day's work to restore that backup; it's just a waste of time.

Luckily, GitLab makes it super easy to restore the backup. Retrieve the backup from your external Amazon S3 storage or just your external hard drive, copy the file to your server, and run the `backup restore` command. It won't get any easier!

Getting ready

Make sure you have a recent backup of your GitLab instance. After you restore the backup, all the data created between the backup creation and the restoration of your backup will be lost.

How to do it...

Let's restore a backup using the following steps:

1. Start with a login to your server using SSH.

   The next few steps concentrate on the GitLab source installation.

2. Go to your `gitlab` folder:

   ```
   $ cd /home/git/gitlab
   ```

3. Go to the backup folder of GitLab:

   ```
   $ cd /home/git/gitlab/tmp/backups
   ```

4. Look at the filename of the most recent file and note the number that the filename starts with.

5. Go back to your GitLab folder:

   ```
   $ cd /home/git/gitlab
   ```

6. Now, run the following command and replace the `1234567` part with the number you took from the latest backup filename:

   ```
   $ bundle exec rake gitlab:backup:restore RAILS_ENV=production
   BACKUP=1234567
   ```

   The next few steps concentrate on the GitLab Omnibus installation.

7. Make sure your backup file is located at `/var/opt/gitlab/backups`:

   ```
   $ cp 1407564013_gitlab_backup.tar /var/opt/gitlab/backups/
   ```

8. Before we can restore the backup, we need to stop our instance. First, stop GitLab itself:

   ```
   $ sudo gitlab-ctl stop unicorn
   ```

9. Next, stop the background worker:

   ```
   $ sudo gitlab-ctl stop sidekiq
   ```

10. Now, we will restore our backup. You need to provide the timestamp of the backup you want to restore. The timestamp is the long number before the filename. Warning: this will overwrite all the data in your database! The following command depicts this:

    ```
    $ sudo gitlab-rake gitlab:backup:restore
    BACKUP=TIMESTAMP_OF_BACKUP
    ```

11. Restoring the actual backup might take a little while depending on the size of your database.

12. Restart your GitLab server again:

    ```
    $ sudo gitlab-ctl start
    ```

Importing an existing repository

It's quite simple to import your repositories from somewhere else. All you need to do is create a new project and select the repository to be imported. In this recipe, we will take a look at how this is done. For this recipe, we will import the repository hosted on GitHub at `https://github.com/gitlabhq/gitlab-shell`.

How to do it...

In the following steps, we will import a repository:

1. Log in to your GitLab instance.

2. Click on **New project**.

3. Enter the project name as `GitLab Shell`.

4. Click on **Import existing repository?**.

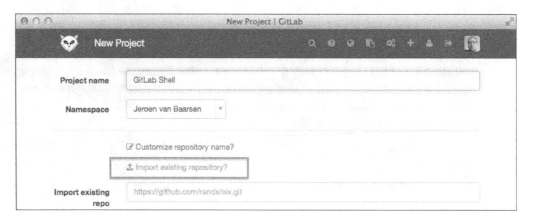

5. Enter the URL for the repository we want to import:

    `https://github.com/gitlabhq/gitlab-shell`

6. Now, click on **Create Project**.

7. Importing the existing repository might take a while depending on the size of the repository.

8. After the importing is done, you will be redirected to the project page.

9. Let's check whether it's actually an imported repository. Click on the **Network** menu item. If everything is fine, you should see the graph in the following screenshot:

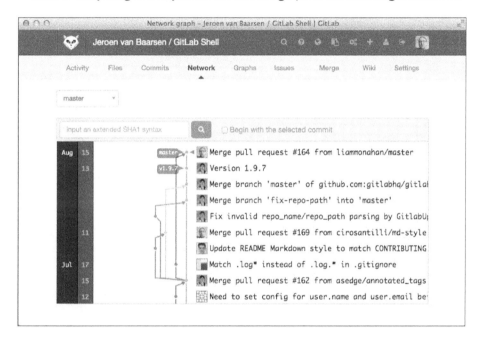

How it works...

There is really nothing magical about importing a repository. All GitLab does is clone the URL you give it to its own satellite. After this is done, the satellite will be linked to your project, and you're done!

What if your repository is private and not publicly accessible? You can import it by adding the user credentials in the URL. Don't worry; this information is not stored anywhere!

So, if we have the same repository as the one we used earlier but it has credentials, it will look like what is shown in `https://username:password@github.com/gitlabhq/gitlab-shell`.

6
Webhooks, External Services, and the API

In this chapter, we will cover the following recipes:

- ▶ Working with external services
- ▶ Using webhooks
- ▶ Using system hooks
- ▶ Getting your private token for the API
- ▶ Understanding the API status codes
- ▶ Managing your project via the API
- ▶ Managing issues via the API
- ▶ Working with the other API resources
- ▶ Working with the API sudo commands

Introduction

When you have an external system that holds information—for example, an external bug tracker—it would be nice to link GitLab and that system together. In this chapter, we will take a look at how you can achieve this. We will also take a look at webhooks in order to notify systems about events happening within your GitLab installation. Finally, we will look at the API provided by GitLab to manage your GitLab system without using the web interface.

Working with external services

GitLab has built-in support for a variety of external services, so you can integrate GitLab with your favorite chat service, such as Slack or Campfire, or project management tools, such as Assembla or Pivotal Tracker. In this recipe, we will take a look at how you can set up GitLab to send out an e-mail when someone pushes a commit.

How to do it...

In the following steps, we will set up e-mails on a push:

1. Log in to your GitLab instance as a project owner.

2. Click on the project for which you want to set up the service. In this example, I'll be using the `super-git` project that was created in a previous chapter.

3. Click on **Settings**.

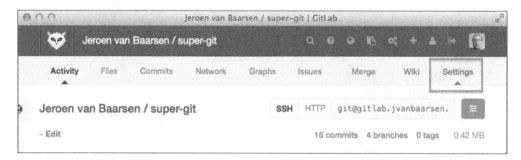

4. Click on **Services** in the left-hand side menu.

5. First, we're going to set up the e-mail on push notifications. Click on **Email on Push**.

6. Check the **Active** checkbox and fill in the e-mail addresses you want GitLab to send mails to.

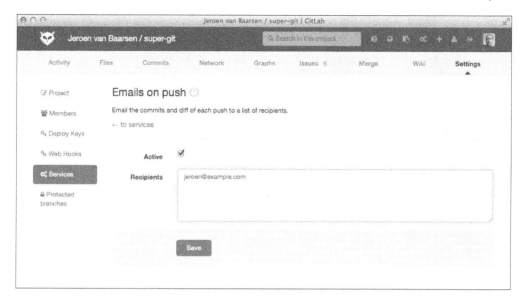

7. Click on **Save**.

8. After you've saved the service, you get a new **Test settings** button.

9. When you go to your mail inbox, you should see a test mail, which looks like the following screenshot:

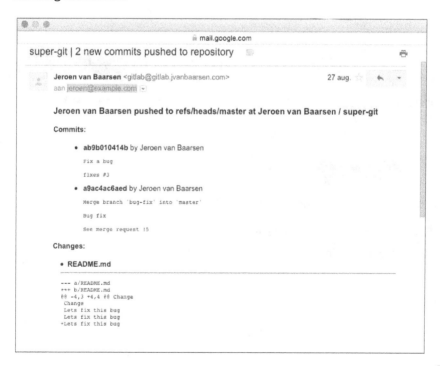

10. Every time you push, the recipients you entered earlier will receive an e-mail about this.

11. There are many more services for you to check out! Most of them require a subscription to an external service.

There's more...

GitLab has a lot of external services you can use. Most of them require you to have an account at a third party. The list of the services is as follows:

- Assembla
- Campfire
- E-mails on Push
- Flowdock
- Gemnasium
- GitLab CI
- HipChat
- Pivotal Tracker
- Slack

When you try to activate a particular service, the page has excellent documentation on the steps you have to take to set up the service.

Using webhooks

GitLab allows you to set up webhooks that will be triggered every time a certain type of event is launched. In this recipe, we will take a look at how you can set up these webhooks yourself and how you can test whether they work without building a complete script around it.

How to do it...

In the following steps, we will configure the webhooks:

1. Log in to your GitLab instance as a project owner.
2. Go to the project for which you want to enable webhooks.

3. Click on **Settings**.

4. Click on **Web hooks** in the left-hand side menu.

5. Here, you see the form that you can use to set up the webhooks. As we won't be writing a script to catch these events, we will be using a web service that enables us to catch the events.

6. As we want to have a place to test the webhook without having to create a lot of software for it, we are going to use a service called `RequestBin`. Go to `www.requestb.in` and click on **Create a RequestBin**.

7. This will give you an endpoint URL, as shown in the following screenshot:

8. Copy the URL and paste it in the **Web hooks** form.

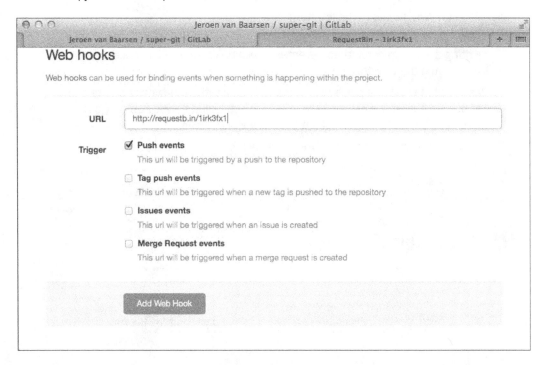

9. For this example, we will be catching all the event types, so check all the boxes under **Trigger** and click on **Add Web Hook**.

10. Your webhook will now be listed under **Web hooks** at the end of the page.

11. You also have a button for testing this hook. Click on **Test Hook**.

12. This will send a testing event to the endpoint we have entered. Let's see whether it works.

13. Go to the endpoint URL on **RequestBin**.

14. If you configured the hook correctly, you should see a test event in **RequestBin**.

RequestBin – 1irk3fx1

Jeroen van Baarsen / super-git | GitLab   RequestBin – 1irk3fx1

http://requestb.in
POST /1irk3fx1
</> application/json
☁ 1.38 kB
51s ago ⚲
From 146.185.139.107

FORM/POST PARAMETERS

None

HEADERS

Connection: close
X-Request-Id: 774d6016-0e76-4c57-81ce-7ed6b384e82e
Content-Type: application/json
Total-Route-Time: 0
Connect-Time: 1
Via: 1.1 vegur
Content-Length: 1416
Host: requestb.in

RAW BODY

{"before":"a2bc24c0141bad528facfabf2d5150b414dc0c9e","after":"a9ac4ac6aede85528bba7bd6646325326d88d869","ref":"refs/heads/master","user_id":2,"user_name":"Jeroen van Baarsen","project_id":1,"repository":{"name":"super-git","url":"git@gitlab.jvanbaarsen.com:jeroen/super-git.git","description":"","homepage":"http://gitlab.jvanbaarsen.com/jeroen/super-git"},"commits":[{"id":"a9ac4ac6aede85528bba7bd6646325326d88d869","message":"Merge branch 'bug-fix' into 'master'\n\nBug fix\n\nSee merge request !5","timestamp":"2014-07-29T15:10:13-04:00","url":"http://gitlab.jvanbaarsen.com/jeroen/super-git/commit/a9ac4ac6aede85528bba7bd6646325326d88d869","author":{"name":"Jeroen van Baarsen","email":"jeroenvanbaarsen@gmail.com"}},{"id":"ab9b010414b3c5be248585456d39b0fac0aa05cd","message":"Fix a bug\n\nfixes #3","timestamp":"2014-07-29T15:09:40-04:00","url":"http://gitlab.jvanbaarsen.com/jeroen/super-git/commit/ab9b010414b3c5be248585456d39b0fac0aa05cd","author":{"name":"Jeroen van Baarsen","email":"jeroenvanbaarsen@gmail.com"}},{"id":"a2bc24c0141bad528facfabf2d5150b414dc0c9e","message":"Merge branch 'another-branch' into 'master'\n\nAnother branch\n\nSee merge request !4","timestamp":"2014-07-29T15:08:03-04:00","url":"http://gitlab.jvanbaarsen.com/jeroen/super-git/commit/a2bc24c0141bad528facfabf2d5150b414dc0c9e","author":{"name":"Jeroen van Baarsen","email":"jeroenvanbaarsen@gmail.com"}}],"total_commits_count":3}

15. You have now successfully configured webhooks.

How it works...

GitLab can send you a few events through the webhook system. You can set up a single webhook to receive all the events, but if you have different systems for different events, that's no problem! This is because you can choose which events you want to send to which webhook.

The events that GitLab currently has hooks for are as follows:

▶ **Push events**: These will be triggered when you push a commit to the repository
▶ **Tag push events**: These will be triggered once a new tag is pushed to the repository
▶ **Issue events**: These will be triggered when an issue is created
▶ **Merge request events**: These will be triggered when a merge request is created

Webhooks are useful, for example, when you have an automatic deploy system in place, someone pushes a new tag, and a deployment has to be triggered. Or, maybe you have a custom chat system that you want to receive a notification for when a new issue has been created.

Using system hooks

When you create or delete a user or project, you might want to be notified, or you might have a backend system from which you want to receive notifications for this type of events. GitLab has support for this in the form of system hooks. In this recipe, we take a look at how you can set up system hooks for your GitLab instance.

The following events can trigger a system webhook call:

▶ Project created
▶ Project destroyed
▶ New team member
▶ The team member is removed
▶ A user is created
▶ The user is removed

How to do it...

In the following steps, we will set up the system hooks:

1. Log in to GitLab as an administrator.
2. Go to the **Admin area** section.

3. Click on **Hooks**.

4. As we want to have a place to test the webhook without having to create a lot of software for it, we are going to use a service called `RequestBin`. Go to `www.requestb.in` and click on **Create a RequestBin**.

5. Copy the URL that is given on that page, and paste it to GitLab in the hook's **URL** field.

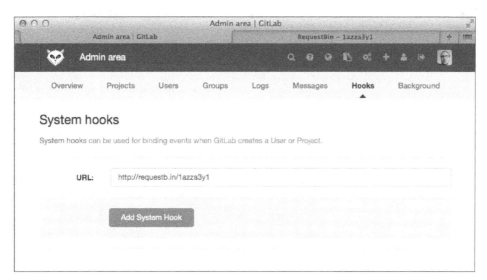

6. When you click on **Add System Hook**, the hook will be added and listed at the bottom of the page. There will also be a button called **Test Hook**. Click on this button so that we can check the data that gets sent to `RequestBin`.

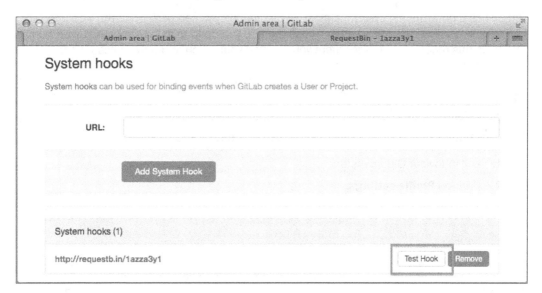

7. If you now go back to **RequestBin**, you see the event getting registered there.

Getting your private token for the API

GitLab has a powerful API system; almost all the actions you can perform in the web interface can also be done via the API. In order to use the API, you need to get your private token from GitLab. In this recipe, we will see where you can find your token and how you can regenerate an existing token.

How to do it...

In the following steps, we will create our private token for the API:

1. Log in to your GitLab instance.
2. Click on **Profile settings**.

3. Click on **Account**.

4. Here, you can find your private token:

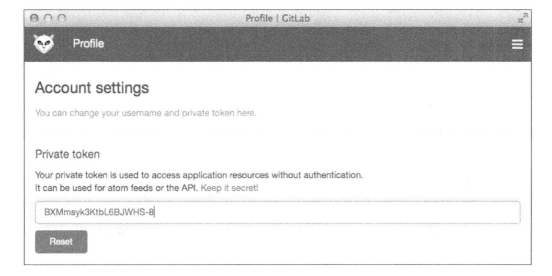

5. If you need to reset your token because it has been compromised, you can do so by clicking on the **Reset** button.

6. GitLab will now generate a new token for you.

How it works...

The private token is used for all the API requests; it's a replacement for the username/password combination. You have to make sure that your private token is kept secure; the same way you have to make sure your username/password is secure.

When you have the feeling your token has been compromised, you need to generate a new one, as the person who has your token can perform all sorts of actions in the GitLab system on your behalf.

Understanding the API status codes

When you start working with the GitLab API, it's good to be aware of the different status codes that can be returned. In this recipe, I'll explain what each status code means and, if possible, how to solve it. The status codes GitLab uses are equivalent to the HTTP standard status codes.

How it works...

GitLab has the following API status codes:

- ▶ 200 − OK: This means that the GET, PUT, or DELETE request was successful. When you request a resource, it will be returned in JSON format.

- ▶ 201 − Created: This means that the POST request was successful. This status code is only returned when you try to create a new resource. The resource will also be returned to you.

- ▶ 400 − Bad Request: This means you have missed a required attribute for this request. For example, the title for a merge request was not given.

- ▶ 401 − Unauthorized: This means that you are not authenticated. If you don't send a secret token with your request or send an invalid token, this status is returned.

- ▶ 403 − Forbidden: This means that you are authenticated but don't have the required permissions to perform the given request. This can happen, for example, if you try to delete a project but you're not an owner of the project.

- ▶ 404 − Not Found: This means that the resource you're trying to fetch does not exist. For example, you try to request an issue by its ID, but that issue could not be found.

- ▶ 405 − Method not allowed: This means that GitLab does not support the request you try to perform.

- ▶ 409 − Conflict: This means that a conflicting resource already exists; for example, you try to create a project with the same name as a project that was already created.

▶ 500 - Server error: This means that something went wrong with your request. This was a server-side issue, so you don't have to alter your message. You might find a bug in GitLab.

Managing your projects via the API

GitLab has a very powerful API. You can manage almost your entire GitLab instance with the API. In this chapter, we are going to take a look at how you can create projects and manage them via the API.

Getting ready

As we won't be writing any real code but just testing the API endpoints, you need a program to test these endpoints. I'll be using Postman for Google Chrome. You can download it from `http://goo.gl/SmDU3j`.

When using the API in production, you don't need to use Postman. I'm only using this to easily test the API. In production, you would use your own application to consume the API.

How to do it...

1. Let's start by retrieving all the projects we currently have in our GitLab server.

2. Open the Postman app and enter your GitLab URL followed by `/api/v3/projects?secret_token=YOUR_TOKEN`.

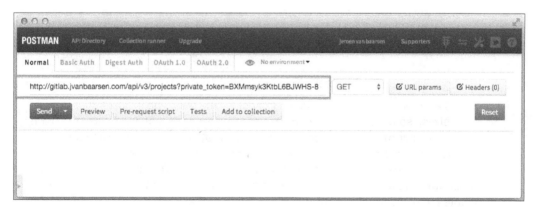

3. When you click on **Send**, the API will be triggered, and you see the response that GitLab is giving you. In this case, you will see a JSON string with all your project data.

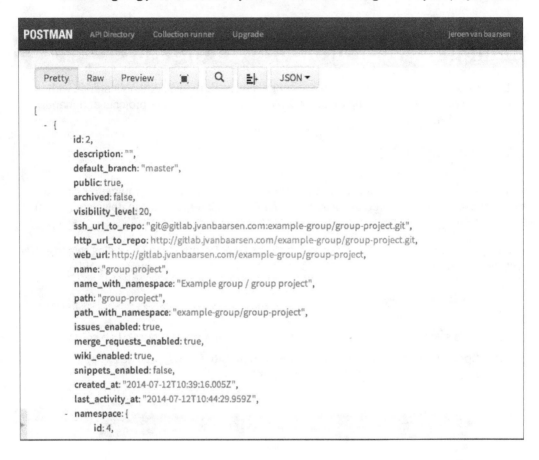

4. Next, we will create a new project via the API.

5. In this example, we will be creating a project for the user who is using the API (ourselves), so we won't need a `user_id` for a user, as GitLab will figure that out by looking at your `private_token` key. We can create a new project using the `POST http://example.com/api/v3/projects?private_token=your_token` endpoint. If you're using Postman, you have to select **POST** from the HTTP method's dropdown. You also have to enter the parameters you want to send to GitLab to create a project; we only need the name, so enter the name. Your view should look like what is shown in the following screenshot:

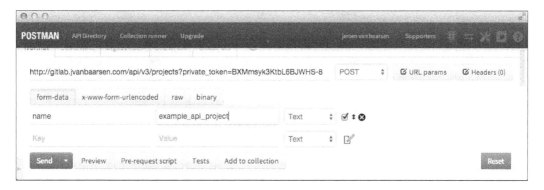

6. If you now click on the **Send** button, your project will be created for you. You know that everything went well if you get back the `201` status code and the newly created project in JSON format.

7. Let's make sure that the project is created by going to our GitLab web interface.

8. Go to **Projects**. You should see the project you've just created in the list.

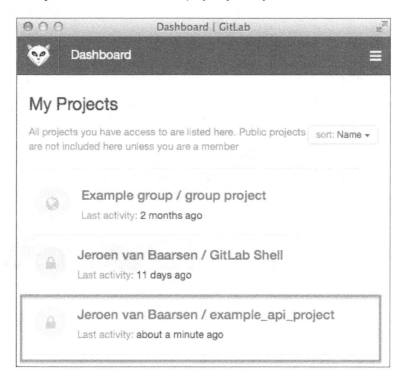

Managing issues via the API

One of the most used features in the GitLab API is the creation and listing of issues for a given project. In this recipe, we will take a look at how you can incorporate this into your own workflow.

Getting ready

You need to have your own `private_token` present, as every call needs this. We will be creating issues for a project, which means that you also need to have at least one project in your GitLab instance.

How to do it...

1. Let's start by getting the `project_id` field for which we want to create the issue. You can do this by entering the `http://example.com/api/v3/projects?private_token=your_token` endpoint in Postman. This will give you a JSON output of all your projects. Just pick one for which you want to create some issues and note the ID.

2. Now that we have the `project_id` field, we can create a new issue via the API. The endpoint requires a few necessary fields, which are the `project_id` field and the title of the issue.

3. To create the actual issue, you need to enter this endpoint in Postman: `http://example.com/api/v3/projects/your_project_id/ issues?private_token=your_token`.

4. Set the HTTP method to **POST** in Postman.

5. Now, fill in the title for the issue in the fields that appeared when you changed the HTTP method. After you've done that, the form should look like what is shown in the following screenshot:

6. When you click on the **Send** button, GitLab will create a new issue for you in the given project.

7. If the issue was created successfully, you get back a `201` HTTP code and a JSON string containing the newly created resource.

8. To verify that this issue has been created successfully, let's get all the issues for the project to see whether our new issue is in there.

9. You can do so by using the `http://example.com/api/v3/projects/your_project_id/issues?private_token=your_token` endpoint. Make sure the HTTP send method is set to **GET**.

10. You should now receive a JSON response that contains all the issues for the given project, including the one we just created.

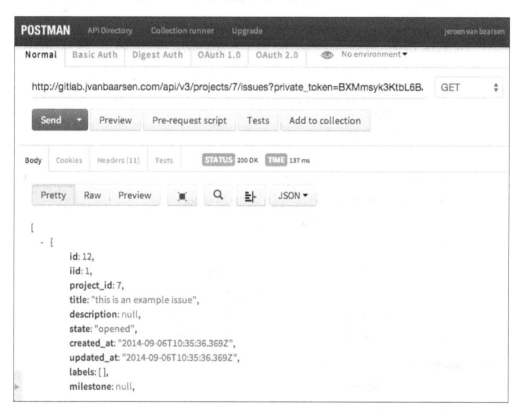

Working with other API resources

GitLab has more resources you can manage via the API. They are as follows:

- **Users**: The following tasks can be performed to manage users:
    - List users
    - Get, create, edit, and delete a user
    - List SSH keys for a given user
    - Get, create, and edit SSH keys for a user

- **Sessions**: These can be managed in the following way:
    - Log in with your e-mail and password to get your private token

- **Projects**: These can be managed in the following ways:
    - List all the projects
    - Get a single project
    - Get project events
    - Create a new project
    - Remove a project
    - List all the team members for a given project
    - Get, create, edit, and delete a team member
    - Get, add, edit, and delete project hooks
    - Get all the branches
    - Get a single branch
    - Protect and unprotect branches

- **Project snippets**: These can be handled in the following ways:
    - Get, create, update, and delete code snippets for a project

- **Repositories**: These can be managed in the following ways:
    - List all the Git tags
    - Create a new Git tag
    - Get a raw file or blob content
    - Compare branches, tags, or commits
    - List all the contributors

► **Commits**: These can be managed in the following ways:

 ❏ List all the commits for a repository

 ❏ Get a single commit

 ❏ Get the difference for a single commit

► **Branches**: These can be managed in the following ways:

 ❏ List, get, create, protect, unprotect, and delete branches

► **Merge requests**: These can be managed in the following ways:

 ❏ List all the merge requests

 ❏ Get, create, edit, accept, and close merge requests

 ❏ Get all the comments for a given merge request

► **Issues**: These can be managed in the following ways:

 ❏ List, get, create, and edit issues

► **Groups**: These can be managed in the following ways:

 ❏ List, get, and create groups

 ❏ Transfer the project to a group

 ❏ List all the group members

 ❏ Add and remove group members

Working with the API sudo command

In GitLab, all API requests you make are completed as the user you're logged in as. As an administrator, you might want to perform a specific action on behalf of one of your users. This can be done by asking them for their `private_token` key, but GitLab has a better way of performing these kind of operations. You can run a command with the `sudo` parameter.

The `sudo` parameter has to be given with capitals, and as a value for this parameter, you have to provide the username for the user.

So, for example, if we want to list all projects but want to do this as the user `John`, our endpoint call will look as follows:

```
http://yourdomain/api/v3/projects?private_token=your_token&SUDO=john
```

If the user given as the `SUDO` parameter is not found, the API will return a `403` code.

7
Using LDAP and OmniAuth Providers

In this chapter, we will look at the following recipes:

- ▶ Setting up your LDAP server
- ▶ Installing a web interface for LDAP
- ▶ Adding a user in your LDAP server
- ▶ Configuring GitLab to use LDAP on an Omnibus installation
- ▶ Configuring GitLab to use LDAP on a source installation
- ▶ Setting up GitHub as an OmniAuth provider

Introduction

In this chapter, we will take a look at how you can use an LDAP server to manage all the users in your GitLab system. This might be useful if you have more systems in your company that already use LDAP; think about e-mails or filesystems.

Another useful thing we will look at is how you can use external authentication methods called OmniAuth providers to allow users to log in using systems from third parties.

Setting up your LDAP server

Before you can link GitLab to your LDAP server, you first have to set up this server. We are going to look at how you can install OpenLDAP on to your Ubuntu machine.

How to do it...

In the following steps, we prepare the server for LDAP:

1. Log in via SSH to your newly installed server.

2. Start by updating the available packages:

   ```
   sudo apt-get update
   ```

3. Install LDAP and some very useful LDAP utilities:

   ```
   sudo apt-get install slapd ldap-utils
   ```

   You will be asked to enter an administrator password.

4. Now, configure our LDAP server. I assume that you have a domain for your LDAP environment. I'll use `ldap.example.com` for the rest of this recipe.

5. Start the configuration tool by running the following command:

   ```
   sudo dpkg-reconfigure slapd
   ```

6. Under the **Omit OpenLDAP server configuration** option, select **No**.

7. Mention your domain as the DNS domain. In my case, this is `ldap.example.com`.

8. Mention your organization name. In my case, this is `example`.

9. Under the **Database backend to use:** option, select **HDB**.

10. Under the option to purge the slapd database, select **No**.

11. Under the **Move old database?** option, select **Yes**.

12. Under the **Allow LDAPv2 protocol** option, select **No**.

You have now installed LDAP on your server.

Installing a web interface for LDAP

As LDAP is not very easy to manage over the terminal, we will install a web interface so that the process of adding users becomes a bit more bearable. The management tool we will be using is called phpLDAPadmin. Other options to manage your LDAP environment are also available; a full list of options is available at `http://en.wikipedia.org/wiki/List_of_LDAP_software`.

How to do it...

Let's install the LDAP server:

1. Perform an SSH into your LDAP server.

2. Install phpLDAPadmin by running the following command:

    ```
    $ sudo apt-get install phpldapadmin
    ```

3. Next, we configure phpLDAPadmin to know about our LDAP server:

    ```
    $ sudo vim /etc/phpldapadmin/config.php
    ```

4. Search for `$servers->setValue('server','name','My LDAP Server');` and change `My LDAP Server` to the name you want to show in the tree view.

5. Search for `$servers->setValue('server','host','127.0.0.1');` and replace the `127.0.0.1` port number with the domain name your LDAP server is running on. In my case, this is `ldap.example.com`.

6. Next, set up the correct domain components. You have to transform your LDAP domain name to a format that LDAP understands. The format LDAP is using for a domain is `dc=example,dc=com`. This means that every part of your domain has to be split and formatted with `dc=`. So, for the `ldap.example.com` domain, this will become `dc=ldap,dc=example,dc=com`.

7. Search for `$servers->setValue('server','base',array('dc=example,dc=com'));` and replace the highlighted part with your own value. In my case, this is `dc=ldap,dc=example,dc=com`.

8. Search for `$servers->setValue('login','bind_id','cn=admin,dc=example,dc=com');` and replace the highlighted part. So, in my case, this will become `$servers->setValue('login','bind_id','cn=admin,dc=ldap,dc=example,dc=com');`.

Now, you can save and close the file. Your phpLDAPadmin tool has been configured successfully.

Adding a user to your LDAP server

Before a user can log in to your GitLab server, they need to have an account in the LDAP server. In this recipe, we will take a look at how you can add groups and users to your LDAP server using the phpLDAPadmin tool.

How to do it...

Let's create a new user:

1. Go to the domain that your LDAP server is running and append `phpldapadmin` to the URL, for example, `http://ldap.example.com/phpldapadmin`.

2. Click on the **login** link and enter your administrator password.

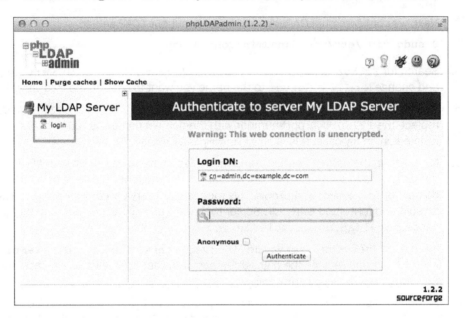

3. First, create a group to house all the users.

4. In the tree view in the left-hand side view, click on the little **+** sign.

5. Click on **Create a new entry here**.

6. Select **Generic: Posix Group**.

7. You will see a screen where you can enter the group name. Enter `Users` and click on **Create Object**.

8. You will see the confirmation window again. Click on **Commit**.

9. Next, create an actual user!

10. Click on the group we just created in the tree view.

11. Click on **Create a child entry**.

12. Select the **Generic: User Account** option.

13. Fill in the form with the information for the user you want to create. In my case, I used the following:

    ❑ **Common name**: John Doe

    ❑ **First name**: John

    ❑ **GID Number**: GitLab_Users

    ❑ **Home directory**: /home/users/jdoe

    ❑ **Last name**: Doe

    ❑ **Login shell**: /bin/sh

    ❑ **User ID**: jdoe

    ❑ **Password**: Something secure

14. Click on **Create Object**.

15. In the confirmation window, click on **Commit**.

16. In order for GitLab to be able to create a correct user object upon the first login, we need to add an e-mail address to this LDAP user.

17. Click on the user in the left-hand side menu.

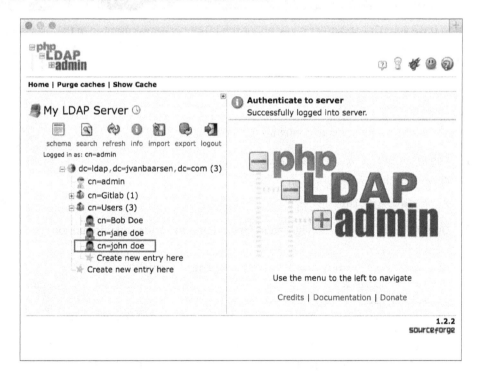

18. Click on **Add new Attribute**.

19. Select **Email** from the drop-down list.

20. Fill in the e-mail address, for example, john.doe@example.com.

21. Scroll down and click on **Update Object**.

22. You see a confirmation screen. Click on **Update Object** again.

You have now created your first LDAP user!

How it works...

As we want to use LDAP for GitLab, this means that you should not be creating users directly in GitLab itself. In this recipe, I've made the choice to store all the user accounts in the Gitlab_Users group, but this is not required. If you feel more comfortable with another user group, that is not a problem.

Configuring GitLab to use LDAP on an Omnibus installation

In order to have your GitLab server know about the LDAP server we created in the previous recipe, we need to configure it. In this recipe, I'll show you how to do this. We will be using GitLab Omnibus in this recipe.

How to do it...

We perform the following steps to configure GitLab to use LDAP:

1. Log in via SSH to your GitLab server.

2. Go to the GitLab configuration folder:

   ```
   $ cd /etc/gitlab/
   ```

3. Open the gitlab.rb configuration file and add the following information:

   ```
   gitlab_rails['ldap_enabled'] = true
   gitlab_rails['ldap_host'] = 'your_ldap_server'
   gitlab_rails['ldap_port'] = 389
   gitlab_rails['ldap_uid'] = 'uid'
   gitlab_rails['ldap_method'] = 'plain' # 'ssl' or 'plain'
   gitlab_rails['ldap_bind_dn'] =
   'CN=admin,DC=your,DC=ldap,DC=server'
   gitlab_rails['ldap_password'] = 'your_ldap_admin_pass'
   gitlab_rails['ldap_allow_username_or_email_login'] = true
   gitlab_rails['ldap_base'] = 'DC=your,DC=ldap,DC=server'
   ```

It is important that you keep an eye on the ldap_base and ldap_bind_dn values. They need to be in a format that LDAP understands. For example, if your domain is ldap.jvanbaarsen.com, the value needs to be 'DC=ldap,DC=jvanbaarsen,DC=com'. If you don't use a subdomain and your domain is jvanbaarsen.com, the value would look like 'DC=jvanbaarsen,DC=com'.

4. Save the file and reconfigure GitLab:

    ```
    $ sudo gitlab-ctl reconfigure
    ```

5. The next step is to verify our work. Go to your GitLab server in the browser. If you configured GitLab correctly, you should see the LDAP tab on the login screen.

6. In the previous recipe, we created a user named jdoe. I think it's time to log in as John Doe! The username for this user is jdoe.

You have now linked your LDAP server to the GitLab server!

Configuring GitLab to use LDAP on a source installation

In this recipe, we will configure your GitLab source installation to use the LDAP server.

How to do it...

We perform the following steps to use LDAP on a source installation:

1. Log in via SSH to your GitLab server.

2. Go to the directory with the gitlab.yml configuration file:

    ```
    $ cd /home/git/gitlab/config/
    ```

3. Open the gitlab.yml file and find the ldap section.

4. Change enabled: false to enabled: true.

5. Change the following information:

    ```
    host: '_your_ldap_server'
    port: 636
    uid: 'uid'
    method: 'plain' # "tls" or "ssl" or "plain"
    bind_dn: 'CN=admin,DC=your,DC=ldap,DC=server'
    password: '_the_password_of_the_bind_user'
    base: 'DC=your,DC=ldap,DC=server'
    ```

It is important that you keep an eye on the `base` and the `bind_dn` values. They need to be in a format that LDAP understands. For example, if your domain is `ldap.jvanbaarsen.com`, the value needs to be `'DC=ldap,DC=jvanbaarsen,DC=com'`. If you don't use a subdomain and your domain is `jvanbaarsen.com`, the value would look like `'DC=jvanbaarsen,DC=com'`.

6. Save the file.

7. To make sure GitLab picks up the changes, we need to restart it:

   ```
   $ sudo service gitlab start
   ```

Setting up GitHub as an OmniAuth provider

When your company is switching to GitLab, chances are that you're using GitHub at this point. So, all of the employees have a GitHub account and might even use that GitHub account to do their own open source work. It would be great if you could make the switch to GitLab without forcing your employees to create a new account. In this recipe, we will take a look at how you can set up GitLab so that your people can authenticate themselves with their GitHub account.

How to do it...

With the following steps, we will register a GitLab app on GitHub and link it to our GitLab server:

1. Log in to your GitHub account.

2. Go to your user settings.

3. Click on **Applications**.

4. Click on **Register new application**.

5. You now see a form that needs to be filled in; let's go over the following fields:

   - **Application name**: This is a new application name that your users will recognize and trust. In my example, I'll use `GitLab Example app`.

   - **Homepage URL**: This is the URL to your GitLab app. In my case, this is `gitlab.example.com`.

   - **Application description**: This is optional and will be shown to your users when they authenticate.

   - **Authorization callback URL**: This is an important field and needs to be in the `your_gitlab_domain/users/auth/github/callback` format. So in my case, this will be `http://gitlab.example.com/users/auth/github/callback/`.

6. Once you're done, the form should look like the following screenshot:

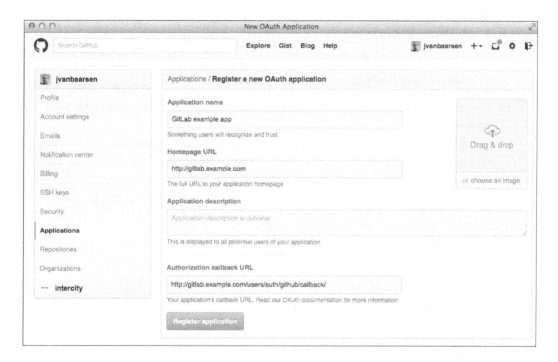

7. When you click on **Register Application**, you will see a page that has the **Client ID** and **Client Secret** values. We need this information later on when we configure our GitLab server. It is important to keep the **Client Secret** value secure, as it allows people to use the app on your behalf. The following screenshot depicts this:

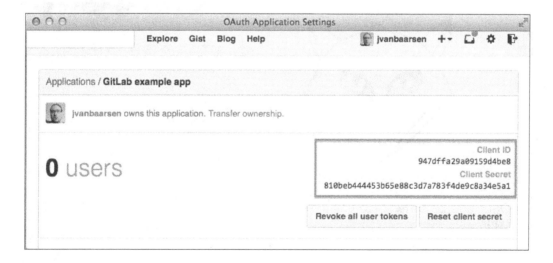

8. Log in via SSH to your GitLab server.

9. Go to the GitLab configuration folder:

    ```
    $ cd /home/git/gitlab
    ```

10. Edit the `gitlab.yml` file at `config/gitlab.yml`:

    ```
    $ sudo -u git -H editor config/gitlab.yml
    ```

11. Find the part about OmniAuth and change the `enabled: false` section to `enabled: true`.

12. Scroll down a little more to the `Providers` section and search for the `GitHub` provider.

13. Uncomment the `GitHub` lines.

14. Change `YOUR_APP_ID` to the `client_id` value from the app we just created.

15. Change `YOUR_APP_SECRET` to the `client_secret` value from the app we just created.

16. Save the file.

17. Restart your GitLab server:

    ```
    $ sudo /etc/init.d/gitlab restart
    ```

18. Browse your GitLab login screen, and you will see that you can now log in using GitHub.

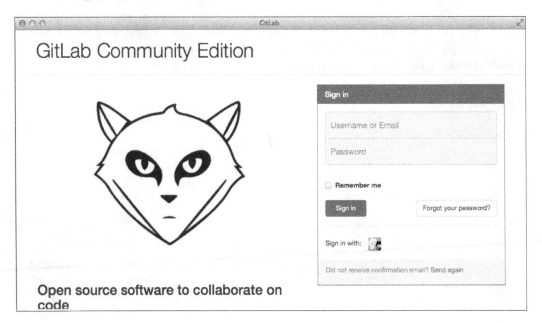

How it works...

GitLab has support for a couple of OmniAuth providers: GitHub, Twitter, and Google. The process of setting up the other providers is the same as that for GitHub; the big difference is the way in which you have to set up the GitLab application on Twitter or Google.

Another thing to keep in mind when setting up the OmniAuth provider is the callback URL; this is also different for every provider and is shown as follows:

- **Twitter**: `your_domain/users/auth/twitter/callback`
- **Google**: `your_domain/users/auth/google_oauth2/callback`

8
GitLab CI

In this chapter, we will cover the following recipes:

- ▸ Installing the dependencies
- ▸ Installing the coordinator
- ▸ Installing the web server
- ▸ Installing a runner
- ▸ Linking your first project to GitLab CI
- ▸ Creating a build script
- ▸ Using GitLab CI webhooks

Introduction to GitLab CI

GitLab CI is a continuous integration solution made by the same team that made GitLab. A CI system allows you to run automated unit tests on every commit, and will warn you when a build is not successful. It is also possible to have a healthy build deployed automatically.

Since the same team that created GitLab created GitLab CI, it has a super nice integration with the GitLab system itself, is a breeze to set up, and is fully integrated in the GitLab interface.

You don't need two different usernames, since the GitLab CI system will work with the API provided by GitLab. Via the API, it can check whether credentials are correct, and whether someone has the right access to certain projects.

The software requirements for GitLab CI are as follows:

- ▶ Ubuntu 12.0.x or Debian/Linux
- ▶ Ruby 1.9.3+
- ▶ GitLab 6.3+
- ▶ MySQL or PostgreSQL

The hardware requirements are as follows:

- ▶ 1 GB of memory is recommended, though 512 MB will work
- ▶ 2 CPU cores or more are recommended, though 1 CPU core will work
- ▶ 100 MB disk space

Installing the dependencies

Before you can install GitLab CI, we need to have some dependencies in place. These dependencies ensure GitLab CI runs smoothly later on in the process. We will install the following dependencies:

- ▶ System packages
- ▶ The Redis server
- ▶ Ruby
- ▶ PostgreSQL

How to do it...

Let's install the dependencies:

1. Log in via SSH to your GitLab server.
2. Let's ensure that our system is up to date using the following command:

   ```
   $ sudo apt-get update && sudo apt-get upgrade
   ```

3. Install the required packages:

   ```
   $ sudo apt-get install wget curl gcc checkinstall libxml2-dev
   $ sudo apt-get install libxslt-dev libcurl4-openssl-dev
   $ sudo apt-get install libreadline6-dev libc6-dev libssl-dev
   $ sudo apt-get install libmysql++-dev make build-essential
   zlib1g-dev
   $ sudo apt-get install openssh-server git-core libyaml-dev
   $ sudo apt-get install redis-server postfix libpq-dev libicu-
   dev
   ```

4. Next, we need to install Ruby using the following commands:

    ```
    $ mkdir /tmp/ruby && cd /tmp/ruby
    $ curl --progress http://cache.ruby-
    lang.org/pub/ruby/2.0/ruby-2.0.0-p353.tar.bz2 | tar xj
    $ cd ruby-2.0.0-p353
    $ ./configure -disable-install-rdoc && make && sudo make
    install
    ```

5. Now that we have installed Ruby, we have to install the package manager for Ruby:

    ```
    $ sudo gem install bundler -no-ri --no-rdoc
    ```

6. For security reasons, we don't want to have the CI server running as the root user. Let's create a new user that will run the CI system:

    ```
    $ sudo adduser -disabled-login -gecos 'GitLab CI' gitlab_ci
    ```

7. GitLab CI can be run using MySQL or PostgreSQL, but since PostgreSQL is the recommended way, I'll use that in this book. Let's install it:

    ```
    $ sudo apt-get install -y postgresql-9.1 libpq-dev
    ```

8. Log in to PostgreSQL:

    ```
    $ sudo -u postgres psql -d template1
    ```

9. Create the GitLab user in PostgreSQL:

    ```
    template1=# CREATE USER gitlab_ci;
    ```

10. Create the database and grant the correct privileges to the GitLab user:

    ```
    template1=# CREATE DATABASE gitlab_ci_production OWNER
    gitlab_ci;
    ```

11. Exit PostgreSQL:

    ```
    template1=# \q
    ```

We have now installed all the dependencies!

Installing the coordinator

The coordinator is the heart of the GitLab CI system. This will let you see all the builds in a web interface, and it will also control the runners, which we will add later. The coordinator doesn't execute any builds. For the purpose of building, we will use decoupled runners. In this recipe, we will install the coordinator, and in the recipe, *Installing a runner*, we will install the runner to run our tests.

How to do it...

In the following steps, we will install the CI coordinator:

1. Log in via SSH to your CI server.

2. Go to the `gitlab_ci` home folder:

   ```
   $ cd /home/gitlab_ci/
   ```

3. Download the source code for the CI server:

   ```
   $ sudo -u gitlab_ci -H git clone https://gitlab.com/gitlab-org/gitlab-ci.git
   $ cd gitlab-ci
   $ sudo -u gitlab_ci -H git checkout 5-0-stable
   ```

4. Now we have the source code, it's time to configure the server. Start by copying the `example config` file:

   ```
   $ sudo -u gitlab_ci -H cp config/application.yml.example config/application.yml
   ```

5. Now, we edit the file to match our GitLab setup:

   ```
   $ sudo -u gitlab_ci -H editor config/application.yml
   ```

6. We need to edit the following values:

   - GitLab server URL
   - GitLab CI Host
   - E-mail from

7. Copy the example web server settings:

   ```
   $ sudo -u gitlab_ci -H cp config/unicorn.rb.example config/unicorn.rb
   ```

8. Create the correct socket and PID directories:

   ```
   $ sudo -u gitlab_ci -H mkdir -p tmp/sockets/
   $ sudo chmod -R u+rwX  tmp/sockets/
   $ sudo -u gitlab_ci -H mkdir -p tmp/pids/
   $ sudo chmod -R u+rwX  tmp/pids/
   ```

9. Now that we have configured the GitLab CI server, we need to install the app dependencies:

   ```
   $ sudo -u gitlab_ci -H bundle install --without development test mysql -deployment
   ```

10. The next step would be to set up the database. Copy the example database config file:

    ```
    $ sudo -u gitlab_ci -H cp config/database.yml.postgresql
    config/database.yml
    ```

11. Set up the database tables:

    ```
    $ sudo -u gitlab_ci -H bundle exec rake setup
    RAILS_ENV=production && sudo -u gitlab_ci -H bundle exec
    whenever -w RAILS_ENV=production
    ```

12. We want the CI server to start automatically when the machine gets restarted. We do this by installing an `init` script:

    ```
    $ sudo cp /home/gitlab_ci/gitlab-
    ci/lib/support/init.d/gitlab_ci /etc/init.d/gitlab_ci
    ```

    ```
    $ sudo update-rc.d gitlab_ci defaults 21
    ```

13. Start the CI server:

    ```
    $ sudo /etc/init.d/gitlab_ci start
    ```

We are done with this part! We have installed the CI server.

Installing the web server

Now that we have installed GitLab CI, we still need a way to expose it to the Internet. This is where Nginx comes into play. In this recipe, we will take a look at how you can set up Nginx to proxy the request back to your GitLab CI app. It is also possible to use another web server such as Apache here, but Nginx is recommended.

How to do it...

In the following steps, we will install the web server:

1. Log in via SSH to your CI server.

2. Install Nginx:

   ```
   $ sudo apt-get install nginx
   ```

3. Next, we have to copy the example site configuration over to the Nginx-enabled sites:

   ```
   $ sudo cp /home/gitlab_ci/gitlab-
   ci/lib/support/nginx/gitlab_ci /etc/nginx/sites-
   enabled/gitlab_ci
   ```

4. We still have to change a few things in the configuration file that we just copied. Change the `default_server` address to the IP address of your server, and change the `server_name` value to the full domain name of your GitLab CI server:

    ```
    $ sudo editor /etc/nginx/sites-enabled/gitlab_ci
    ```

5. Check whether the Nginx configuration is correct:

    ```
    $ sudo nginx -t
    ```

6. Now that we have configured everything, let's start the server:

    ```
    $ sudo /etc/init.d/nginx start
    ```

7. Go to the domain of your CI server to validate whether everything is working correctly.

Installing a runner

Since GitLab CI is created in a way such that it distributes all the builds over more machines, we have to install a so-called runner. A runner is nothing more than a build instance. There can be multiple runners on one machine, but it's also possible to move these runners away to other servers. The ideal situation would be to have one server as the coordinator (hosting the CI web app and controlling the runners) and at least one other server to run one or more runners.

How to do it...

We perform the following steps to install the runner:

1. Log in via SSH to your runner server.

2. Start by updating the `apt-get` repository:

    ```
    $ sudo apt-get update -y
    ```

3. Now, we install all the dependencies:

    ```
    $ sudo apt-get install -y wget curl gcc libxml2-dev
    $ sudo apt-get install libxslt-dev libcurl4-openssl-dev
    $ sudo apt-get install libreadline6-dev libc6-dev libssl-dev
    $ sudo apt-get install make build-essential zlib1g-dev
    openssh-server
    $ sudo apt-get install git-core libyaml-dev postfix libpq-dev
    libicu-dev
    ```

4. Next, we need to install Ruby:

    ```
    $ mkdir /tmp/ruby && cd /tmp/ruby
    $ curl --progress ftp://ftp.ruby-lang.org/pub/ruby/2.0/ruby-
    2.0.0-p353.tar.gz | tar xz & cd ruby-2.0.0-p353
    ```

```
$ ./configure --disable-install-rdoc
$ make
$ sudo make install
```

5. Install the Ruby `bundler` gem:

    ```
    $ sudo gem install bundler
    ```

6. We want the runner to run as its own user, so let's create this user:

    ```
    $ sudo adduser --disabled-login --gecos 'GitLab CI Runner'
    gitlab_ci_runner
    ```

7. Log in as the newly created user:

    ```
    $ sudo su gitlab_ci_runner
    $ cd ~/
    ```

8. We now have all the dependencies installed. Let's install the actual code:

    ```
    $ git clone https://gitlab.com/gitlab-org/gitlab-ci-runner.git
    && cd gitlab-ci-runner
    ```

9. Install all the gems for the runner:

    ```
    $ bundle install –deployment
    ```

10. Set up the runner. This will ask you for a few things:

    ❑ **The coordinator URL**: This is the URL of your GitLab CI app

    ❑ **The token for this runner**: This can be found at `gitlab_ci_domain/admin/runners`

    The command used is as follows:

    ```
    $ bundle exec ./bin/setup && exit
    ```

11. We want the runner to automatically start whenever the server restarts. We can do this by creating the correct `init.d` file:

    ```
    $ cd /home/gitlab_ci_runner/gitlab-ci-runner
    $ sudo cp ./lib/support/init.d/gitlab_ci_runner
    /etc/init.d/gitlab-ci-runner
    $ sudo chmod +x /etc/init.d/gitlab-ci-runner
    $ sudo update-rc.d gitlab-ci-runner defaults 21
    ```

12. The last thing that we need to do is to start the runner:

    ```
    $ sudo service gitlab-ci-runner start
    ```

Linking your first project to GitLab CI

In order to use your GitLab projects in GitLab CI, you need to tell the system that you want to link them together. In this recipe, we will add your project to GitLab CI.

How to do it...

In the following steps, we will add the project to GitLab CI:

1. Go to your GitLab CI web interface.

2. Log in as an admin user.

3. On the root page, you should see a list of your projects. If not, click on the **Sync now** button. The list should look something like the following screenshot:

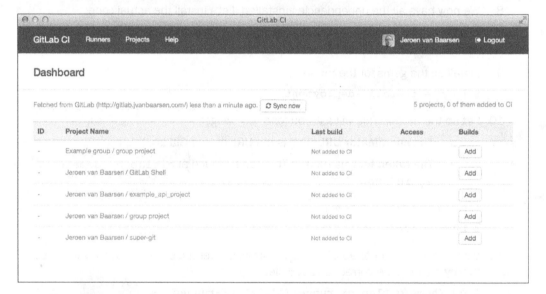

4. To add the project, click on the **Add** button. In this example, I'll add the `super-git` project.

5. When you go to your dashboard, you should be able to see one project that has a yellow background. This means that the project has been added but no build has run yet, so a status cannot be determined.

6. As every project needs at least one runner, let's make sure that the runner is set either to **Shared** or to this project specifically.

7. In the main menu, click on **Runners**.

8. Find the runner that you want to use for this project, of the badge say **Shared**, and you're good to go. If the badge says **Specific**, you need to click on the **Assign to All** button.

Creating a build script

In order to have GitLab CI build your projects, you need to tell it how to build the project. In this example, we will take a look at how you can easily set up a build script. I'll use a web app build on Ruby on Rails. If you use another programming language, you have to create a different build script.

Getting ready

For this recipe, I'll be using the `passty` project made by Dmitriy Zaporozhets, the creator of GitLab. The `passty` project is a web-based password management tool. You can find the project on `https://github.com/randx/passty`. You need to import this project on your own GitLab server. The `passty` project is just an arbitrary example.

How to do it...

1. First, we need to make sure that all the dependencies for this project are installed.

2. Log in via SSH to your GitLab CI server.

3. Let's install SQLite:

    ```
    $ wget http://www.sqlite.org/2014/sqlite-autoconf-
    3080600.tar.gz
    $ sudo tar xvfz sqlite-autoconf-3080600.tar.gz
    $ cd sqlite-autoconf-3080600
    $ sudo ./configure --prefix=/usr/local
    $ sudo make
    $ sudo make install
    ```

4. Log in to your GitLab CI web interface.

5. Click on **Add** for the `passty` project. Remember to click on **Sync now** if you don't see it.

6. Click on **Settings**.

7. You now see a page where you can set up this GitLab CI project.

8. In the box where you can add the build steps, you place this code:

```
cp config/database.yml.sqlite config/database.yml
gem install bundler
bundle install
bundle exec rake db:create RAILS_ENV=test
bundle exec rake db:migrate RAILS_ENV=test
rake test
```

9. Now, go to your GitLab interface and find the project `passty`.

10. Click on **Settings**.

11. Go to **Services**.

12. Find the GitLab CI service. If everything is OK, you should see a green circle on the right.

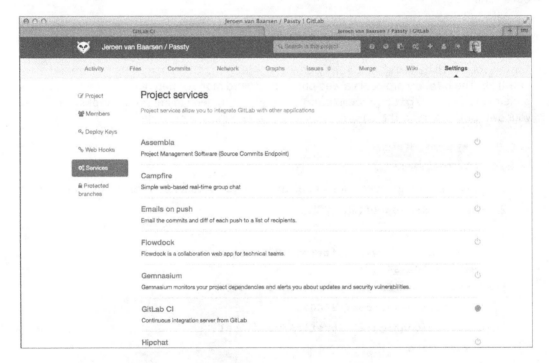

13. Click on the **GitLab CI** link.

14. You will now see a form with all the information of this service. Click on the **Test Settings** link. This will trigger a build of the last commit in GitLab CI.

15. Go back to your GitLab CI interface. If everything went according to plan, the `passty` project should be green now. This means that the project has been built successfully and all the tests have passed, as shown in the following screenshot:

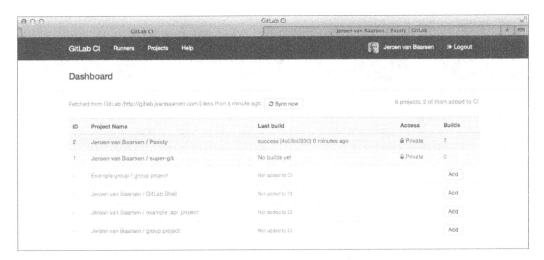

How it works...

When setting up a build, you can choose to set up all the dependencies in the build step itself. This will slow down the build a bit. Or, if the dependencies don't change that often, you can preinstall the dependencies. The latter idea is the one that we have used in this recipe.

I think it's a good practice to configure one runner per application you want to run on GitLab CI, and my experience with this method is that it's easy to add a new runner without having to think about dependency conflicts in the process.

There's more...

You can use GitLab CI to test your code, but it is also possible to check your code, and if the code was successfully built, then you can deploy it to your production environment.

In this way, a feature will get released super fast, and your customers will have the newest features at their fingertips in no time!

There is one requirement for autodeploying your code. When you deploy your code to the live environment, this has to be doable by the commands on the terminal. You can then enter these commands in the **Build Steps** box on the project settings page.

Since deploying your code is very project-specific, I can't give a code snippet that will work in all cases. But if you're writing a Ruby on Rails application, and you deploy your code using Capistrano, it can be done by appending the `cap production deploy` command. As the build will stop once any command in the build steps fails, the code will only be deployed when the build was successful.

Using GitLab CI webhooks

It is possible to have GitLab CI call a webhook whenever a build is run. Setting this up is really straightforward.

How to do it...

Let's set up the webhook with the following steps:

1. Log in to your GitLab CI app as an administrator.
2. Click on the project you want to have webhooks enabled for.
3. Go to the webhooks page.
4. Here, you find an input field where you can enter the URL for the webhook.
5. Click on **Add web hook**.
6. This will add an entry to the enabled webhooks.
7. To test whether the webhook is sending the correct information, you can click on the **Test Hook** button. This will send a sample message to the configured webhook.

How it works...

By configuring the webhook, you can receive notifications about the build status of your commits. This can be a system that checks the incoming message to see whether the build was successful, and if it was, it can deploy the build to a staging or production server.

You can also use the information provided by the webhook to create statistics about the health of your application, and for how many broken builds there were for a given period of time. The possibilities are endless!

Tips and Tricks

In this appendix, we will look at some smaller tasks, tips, and tricks that can help you in your daily GitLab usage.

The power of snippets

Whenever you want to store a little piece of code or just want to share it, you might wonder where you're going to store it. GitLab tries to solve this issue by providing something called snippets. Snippets are little pieces of code that get stored along with the project.

Snippets are disabled by default. To enable them, go to the project settings page, and at the bottom under the heading **Features**, you see a checkbox for **Snippets**. Click on it and save the changes.

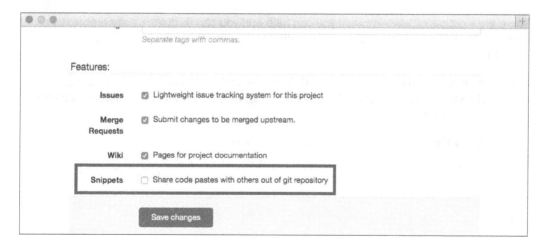

You now have a new menu item called **Snippets**, as shown in the following screenshot. When you go to that page, you see a button to add a new snippet. Once you've added the snippet, it will allow people in the project to see it and also comment on the snippet.

Getting involved

If you have been using GitLab for a while and have decided that you want to help out with this project, you're more than welcome!

There are a couple of ways in which you can help out: you can fix bugs, create new features, help with the issue tracker, and you can also help out with other users in the IRC channel or on Gitter.

At the moment, GitLab is hosted on both GitLab and GitHub. The GitLab version is the canonical source. This means that issues and merge requests are in two different locations, which are as follows:

▸ **GitLab**: `https://gitlab.com/gitlab-org/gitlab-ce`
▸ **GitHub**: `https://github.com/gitlabhq/gitlabhq/`

You can find the IRC channel on freenode. The channel is `#gitlab`. James Newton, Drew Blessing, and Sam Gleske are managing this IRC channel.

The Gitter room is at `https://gitter.im/gitlabhq/gitlabhq`.

When you decide to write a new feature, a good starting point would be to see whether the core team has flagged a certain feature as **Accepting Merge Requests**. You can do this at `http://feedback.gitlab.com`. It is important that you do this as this will provide a chance for your merge requests to be accepted on a bigger scale.

Getting help

Running GitLab can go wrong sometimes. Perhaps something produced an error and you're not sure how to fix this, or maybe you have hit a bug that you want to report. To get help, there are a couple of places you can go to.

The first one is useful if you have a question about how to perform certain tasks, for example, if you get a permission-denied error, invisible repos, or can't clone or push, and so on, you can post them on StackOverflow at `http://stackoverflow.com/questions/tagged/gitlab`. You can also subscribe to the mailing list at `https://groups.google.com/forum/#!forum/gitlabhq`.

If you find a bug, you can report the bug to `https://gitlab.com/gitlab-org/gitlab-ce`. Please keep posting there for actual bugs. If you have a feature request, you can post it to `http://feedback.gitlab.com/`.

If you want to talk to a power user about how to perform certain tasks in general, you can always hop into the Gitter chat room at `https://gitter.im/gitlabhq/gitlabhq`.

The GitLab RSS feed

If you like to receive updates about your projects in your mailbox or other RSS readers, you can. On the dashboard, there is an RSS link called **News Feed**. When subscribing to this RSS feed, you get updates about the issues created, comments placed, and merge requests opened, as shown in the following screenshot:

Archiving projects

When you're working on a lot of projects, some of them might go stale after a while. To prevent this, if you have your GitLab filled with old projects, you can archive these projects.

An archived project is a read-only repository, which means that you cannot push new commits to it, but it is still possible to open issues for this repository.

In order to archive a project, you go to the project settings page and click on the **Dangerous Settings** option. This will expand a few more options. The first option is **Archive project**. Click on this button.

When you go to the project page now, you see a yellow block that tells you that the project has been archived, as shown in the following screenshot. If you need to work on this project, you can unarchive it by going to the **Settings** page. Click on the **Dangerous Settings** option, and then click on **Unarchive**.

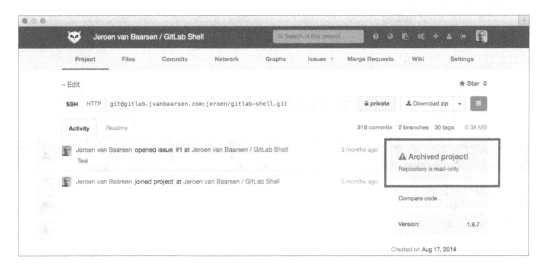

How to format a good Git commit message

When writing a commit message, it is important to tell a story. Why did you make this change? What is it trying to solve? This way, people in the future can see exactly what your intentions were.

There are a few rules you can stick to that will make sure you have the best commit message in your team! They are as follows:

- The first line should contain 50 characters or less and explain the change very briefly.

- The next paragraph should contain a bit more explanation about what you are trying to solve. Try to keep the length of the line under 72 characters; this way, it's easy to scan people.

- If you have more information that you want to tell, you can do so in the next paragraph. This can be as long and detailed as you want. More details are better!

- If you want to create a list, use the – or * characters to do so.

- When you're working on an issue, add a reference to that issue in the last line.

An example of a nicely formatted Git commit message is as follows:

```
Show an error page if the user is not logged in

When a user is not logged in, we do not show an error message.
This was confusing to some users. We now show the correct error
message.

* Here is some extra information
* And here is some more bullet information

Fixes: #1123
```

How to change your Git editor

When you create a Git commit with `git commit -a`, the default editor that will be opened is Vim. This can be very confusing for people, as Vim is not an easy editor if you have never worked with it previously.

Luckily, Git allows you to change the editor that gets opened by default very easily!

There are two ways in which this can be done. The first is via the terminal; this is useful if you want your editor to be Nano, for example. The command to do this is `git config --global core.editor "nano"`. You can change the highlighted section with your editor of choice!

Another way to do this is to edit the `.gitconfig` file in your `home` directory. The location of this file depends on the operating system you're using. The possible locations are as follows:

> ▸ **Windows**: `C:/users/your_username/`
> ▸ **Linux / Mac OS X**: `/home/your_username`

When you open this file in your favorite editor, you need to find the following line:

```
[core]
        editor = 'vim'
```

It might be possible that this line is not yet present in the file; in that case, you need to add it. You can change `vim` to your favorite editor. When you save and close the file and try to perform a Git commit, you will have your own editor!

Understanding the anatomy of GitLab

GitLab is a complex system; it has a lot of moving parts. It's very useful to understand the architecture of GitLab.

At the core of GitLab is the GitLab web app. This is what you see and use everyday. This web app is built upon the Ruby on Rails framework. The database it connects to depends on your configuration, but GitLab advises you to use PostgreSQL.

GitLab is not directly connected to the Web, but it needs an app server and a web server to connect to the outside world. For the app server, Unicorn is used. For the web server, GitLab uses either Nginx or Apache; the GitLab team advises you to use Nginx.

There are a lot of things that need to run in the background. For example, when you push a commit to GitLab, it needs to check whether you referenced an issue or a merge request, and if you did, GitLab needs to create a comment on that item. In order to make all of this work, GitLab uses a background worker called Sidekiq; every item that needs to be processed is called a job. You can see what jobs are being processed by Sidekiq by visiting `http://gitlab.example.com/admin/background_jobs`. You need to be an admin in order to see this page.

GitLab also needs to talk to Git. In order to simplify this, the GitLab team has created a layer over Git that is called GitLab Shell. This means that GitLab does not talk directly to any of your Git repositories but always uses GitLab Shell to do so. GitLab Shell is also responsible for queuing the jobs in Sidekiq.

There is one last component that is important: the Gitlab satellites. For every project you have running on GitLab, the system creates a copy; these copies are called satellites. When you try to merge a merge request, GitLab will check the satellite to see whether the merge request is actually mergeable. It also uses the satellites for the web editor.

To make everything a little more easy to understand, I have created a very simplified schema of the architecture.

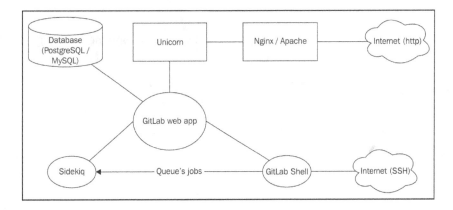

Understanding the differences between GitLab's Community Edition (CE) and Enterprise Edition (EE)

GitLab offers two different versions: the **Community Edition** (**CE**) and the **Enterprise Edition** (**EE**). They offer the same excellent Git hosting, but the difference is in the support you get by GitLab B.V. and the enterprise support.

At the time of writing this, GitLab B.V. offers the following support packages:

- **Basic**: This package costs $19.90 per user/year. It is sold in multiples of 20 users. It provides the following features:
    - Access to GitLab EE
    - Next business-day support

- **Standard**: This package costs $49.00 per user/year. It is sold in multiples of 100 users. It provides the following features:
    - Everything from basic
    - 24/7 emergency support
    - Live installation and configuration assistance
    - Live upgrade assistance
    - High Availability configuration
    - GitLab CI support

- **Plus**: This package costs $249.00 per user/year. It is sold in multiples of 100 users. It provides the following features:
    - Everything from standard
    - Prioritized features that are important to you
    - Best practices and training

GitLab EE also has better support for LDAP, Git hooks, and more. See the following table for the differences between the CE and EE packages:

Differences	CE	EE
All the features of the CE	*	*
Groups consisting of multiple people with a shared namespace for projects	*	*

Differences	CE	EE
Share a project with other groups		*
LDAP user authentication	*	*
Multiple LDAP server support		*
LDAP group sync		*
Create and remove admins based on an LDAP group		*
Git hooks		*
Branded login page		*
Audit events		*
Mention a JIRA ticket from GitLab	*	*
Close JIRA issues with GitLab commits		*
Display the merge request status for builds on the Jenkins CI		*
The omnibus package supports the configuration of an external PostgreSQL database	*	*
The omnibus package supports the configuration of an external MySQL database		*
The omnibus package supports log forwarding		*
An admin can e-mail all users of a project, group, or the entire server		*

How to fork a project and what is forking?

When working with a team on a project, you might not want everyone to push to the main source of the project. You'd rather have everyone create their own copy of the project, commit to their project, and ask whether their code can be merged to the main source of the project.

All this can be achieved by forking a project. You can fork a project in GitLab by going to the project and clicking on the **Fork** button. This will create a copy of the project in your own namespace. You're allowed to do whatever you want with this copy as it's is your own. When you want to push code you created back to the main source, you can create a merge request from your fork back to the main source.

Let's put this in some simple steps:

1. Go to the project you want to fork.
2. In the top-right corner, you see a link called **Fork**. Click on it.

3. GitLab will show you a notice that the project was successfully cloned.

You can now clone this project to your computer and make changes to it. After you're finished with these changes, you can push the code to this fork and create a merge request, just like we did in *Chapter 4, Issue Tracker and Wiki*.

Understanding the branching workflow

When you start using Git, you might be tempted to push all your code directly to the `master` branch. This might not be very good for multiple reasons, one of them being that you can't experiment with new features very well as you pushed everything to `master`. You can't simply delete the branch and start over.

The branching workflow tries to solve this by making sure that the `master` branch is always the latest stable code, and it has to be deployable at all time. So, only code that has been tested and proven to work can go in there.

Let me explain this a bit further.

When you start working on a new feature, you create a new branch, which is named after the feature you're working on. This branch is separate from the `master` branch as that is the latest stable version of the code. You directly push this new branch to GitLab and create a merge request for it. This way, your team knows what you're working on, and it allows them to comment on the thing you're working on from the word go, preventing you from working on something that might now be important or maybe something someone else is working on.

You create new code and, maybe, delete some old code till you're happy with the feature you're working on. To test this code, you deploy this branch to a staging server for you and the team to test out. In the meantime, a team member can review your code in the merge request you created.

Once this code is tested on the staging server and has been reviewed by another team member, it can be merged to `master` and deployed to production.

However, it is also possible that the solution you're trying out doesn't turn out to be the best. When other team members were trying it out, they find that it was not easy to use or a lot of corner cases were found. After discussing with the team, you decided that this feature is not working and you want to delete it. At this point, it's just as simple as closing the merge request without merging and deleting the branch. No need to revert any code. Just delete it and you're done.

Index

H

hardware requisites, GitLab CI 130

I

installation, GitLab
  from Omnibus 8
  from source 11-14
installation, web interface
  for LDAP 118, 119
internal projects 19
issues
  creating 61-63
  managing, via API 112
  managing, ways 115
  referencing 72-76

L

LDAP
  web interface, installing for 118, 119
LDAP server
  setting up 117, 118
  user, adding to 119-122

M

management options, LDAP environment
  URL 118
mention methods, GitLab
  !123 75
  #123 75
  $123 75
  @all 75
  [file](path/to/file) 75
  @user_name 75
  b23cf08 75
merge request
  about 64
  accepting 68-71
  creating 64-68
  managing, ways 115
milestones
  creating 76, 77
  working with 78, 79

O

OmniAuth provider
  GitHub, setting up as 124-127
OmniAuth provider, Google callback
  URL 127
OmniAuth provider, Twitter callback
  URL 127
Omnibus
  used, for installing GitLab 8
Omnibus installation
  updating 86, 87
Omnibus package
  using 8, 9

P

packages, GitLab
  basic 148
  plus 148
  standard 148
passty project
  about 137
  URL 137
phpLDAPadmin 118
Postman, for Google Chrome
  URL, for downloading 109
private projects 19
private token
  creating, for API 106-108
project
  archiving 144
  creating 19, 20
  forking 149, 150
  linking, to GitLab CI 136, 137
  managing, via API 109-111
  managing, ways 114
  types 56
  visibility, configuring 57-59
project snippets
  managing, ways 114
public projects 19

Thank you for buying
GitLab Cookbook

About Packt Publishing

Packt, pronounced 'packed', published its first book "*Mastering phpMyAdmin for Effective MySQL Management*" in April 2004 and subsequently continued to specialize in publishing highly focused books on specific technologies and solutions.

Our books and publications share the experiences of your fellow IT professionals in adapting and customizing today's systems, applications, and frameworks. Our solution based books give you the knowledge and power to customize the software and technologies you're using to get the job done. Packt books are more specific and less general than the IT books you have seen in the past. Our unique business model allows us to bring you more focused information, giving you more of what you need to know, and less of what you don't.

Packt is a modern, yet unique publishing company, which focuses on producing quality, cutting-edge books for communities of developers, administrators, and newbies alike. For more information, please visit our website: www.packtpub.com.

About Packt Open Source

In 2010, Packt launched two new brands, Packt Open Source and Packt Enterprise, in order to continue its focus on specialization. This book is part of the Packt Open Source brand, home to books published on software built around Open Source licenses, and offering information to anybody from advanced developers to budding web designers. The Open Source brand also runs Packt's Open Source Royalty Scheme, by which Packt gives a royalty to each Open Source project about whose software a book is sold.

Writing for Packt

We welcome all inquiries from people who are interested in authoring. Book proposals should be sent to author@packtpub.com. If your book idea is still at an early stage and you would like to discuss it first before writing a formal book proposal, contact us; one of our commissioning editors will get in touch with you.

We're not just looking for published authors; if you have strong technical skills but no writing experience, our experienced editors can help you develop a writing career, or simply get some additional reward for your expertise.

open source
community experience distilled

GitLab Repository Management

ISBN: 978-1-78328-179-4   Paperback: 88 pages

Delve into managing your projects with GitLab, while tailoring it to fit your environment

1. Understand how to efficiently track and manage projects.

2. Establish teams with a fast software developing tool.

3. Employ teams constructively in a GitLab environment.

Gitolite Essentials

ISBN: 978-1-78328-237-1   Paperback: 120 pages

Leverage powerful branch and user access control with Git for your own private collaborative repositories

1. Learn to manage the many repositories and the users accessing these repositories in the Git server.

2. Walks you through the most important ideas and concepts in Gitolite supported by examples and use cases.

3. Master the most powerful tool for fine-grained access control of Git repositories.

Please check **www.PacktPub.com** for information on our titles

Learning Gerrit Code Review

ISBN: 978-1-78328-947-9   Paperback: 144 pages

Leverage the power of Gerrit Code Review to make software development more cooperative and social

1. Understand the concepts of collective code review using Gerrit through a set of simple examples.

2. Integrate code review functionality into Continuous Integration with Jenkins.

3. Experiment with the code review lifecycle in real-life scenarios.

Git Version Control Cookbook

ISBN: 978-1-78216-845-4   Paperback: 340 pages

90 hands-on recipes that will increase your productivity when using Git as a version control system

1. Filled with practical recipes that will teach you how to use the most advanced features of the Git system.

2. Improve your productivity by learning to work faster, more efficiently, and with more confidence.

3. Discover tips and tricks that will show you when and how to use the advanced features of Git.

Please check **www.PacktPub.com** for information on our titles